A Bit of a Caper

By Martin Shipley

Best wishes
Martin Shipley
& Laureen

North Staffordshire Press

North Staffordshire Press

Newcastle-under-Lyme

Staffordshire

A Bit of a Caper

All Rights Reserved

ISBN 978-1-9998703-2-4

First published in 2018

By

North Staffordshire Press

Brampton Business Centre

10 Queen Street

Newcastle-under-Lyme

ST5 1ED

To Maureen for being there every step of the way
and in memory of Dawn, forever in our thoughts.

Acknowledgements

For the incredible support received before, during and after our 'Caper', I would like to give sincere thanks to the following:

Our very dear neighbours Brian and Denise, who looked after our home during the 11 weeks we were away, posted packages of maps to us at key points in our journey and met up with us in Winchester with fresh supplies of clothes and even more maps!

Guy Procter and the team at Country Walking Magazine, whose published articles covering our walk undoubtedly led to the brilliant following we've had on social media. The daily words of encouragement from contributors helped immensely, especially when the going got tough.

Alan Walker and his team at Cotswolds Outdoors Nottingham, for their great gear advice before the walk and for sending gear out to us on route when we needed it.

Our amazing family members and friends who went out of their way to -

Walk with us for one or more days - Dave Kidd, Dave and Lisa Michie, Julian and Wendy Barron, Jo and Tom Dalton, Angie and Gary Owen, Jane Lenton and Chris Smith, Sally Oakley-Qajar and Becky Wells.

Undertake baggage transfers to our next accommodation, providing several days of respite from carrying two full rucksacks - Lesley Sherman, (Tee) Anne Stewart, Rupert Hutchinson, Lindsay Lewis, Frances Ipson, Lindsay Pulley, Helen Taylor, Diane Chadwick, Gaynor Davies, Kate Arthur and Tim Dalton.

Both walk with us and undertake baggage transfers - Pam Clark, Keren Rees, Jacqueline Gale, Nicola Godin, Bev Wood and Andrew White.

Meet up with us, support us or help us in some way - John and Margaret Cutler, Simon and Jacqui Barker, Bryan Shipley, Evie Dalton and Diana Turley.

A mention too for the unsung heroes, the B&B owners, who without them doing what they do would condemn us to 78 nights under canvas, which is just not our thing! Grateful thanks to Alexandra Thomson at Aiden House, Durness, for a brilliant start to our walk and Gordon and Yvonne McNaughton at Torbeckhill B&B, for being there in our hour of need and for a great stay.

We're especially grateful to Maureen's Auntie Jean and Uncle Jack Oates, who in now entering their 80's are an inspiration for 'keeping going'. As well joining us in Shropshire for two of the longest walking days, they travelled down to meet us in Dover at our journey's end and gave us a ride home to Derby.

Grateful thanks also go to our many sponsors, whose generosity helped us to raise much needed funds for our chosen charity, Thrombosis UK.

But most of all I'm immensely proud of my wonderful wife Maureen, who went along (not for the first time) with my wild idea for a walk and who endured the tremendous effort needed, along with a good deal of personal discomfort, to make a walking dream come true.

About the Author

Martin Shipley first became interested in long-distance walking after a fantastic week's holiday in the Lake District, in perfect weather, during the summer of 2003.

This inspired him, together with his wife Maureen, to complete coast-to-coast walks across England (Wainwright's C2C – 2004), Scotland (Southern Upland Way – 2005) and Wales (Offa's Dyke – 2006).

Other significant walks have included the Herriot Way (2006), Dales Way (2007), Glyndwrs Way (2010), John O'Groats to Land's End (2012) and the Tour de Mont Blanc (2015).

They are working their way through Wainwright's 214 Lakeland summits, while Martin is progressing towards completing all 19 current Nationals Trails.

Now retired, Martin and Maureen live on the outskirts of Derby and have between them 4 children and 13 grand-children.

Contents

Chapter 1 - Best Laid Plans

"So, what are you guys getting up to next year?" our friends would ask. "We're going for a bit of a walk", we'd reply. "We're starting at Cape Wrath, the most north-westerly point of the UK and walking to Dover, the most south-easterly point. It's 1,041 miles and we'll do it in 78 days".

Their next question was usually much shorter.

"Why?" they'd ask.

"Remember in 2012 we walked John O'Groats to Lands End? After that we both felt we wouldn't want JOGLE, as it's called, to be the last long distance walk we'd do of that magnitude. So, I looked for options and came up with the idea of walking the 'opposite corners' as it were. Initial research also suggested that no-one has ever done it before, so there's the added appeal of being would-be pioneers!"

The first task had been to design the route. We wanted to take in the dramatic scenery of Cape Wrath and the Kyle of Durness, the glorious mountains and lochs of Scotland, the delights of the Lake District, the drama of Pendle Hill and Lancashire, the classic countryside of Middle England and the Cotswolds, the rolling hills of the Downs and the unique white cliffs of the South Downs. Six months later an outline route was in place. Over the subsequent 2-3 years the finer route details were meticulously mapped out and the logistics carefully planned.

The walk would require 55 Ordnance Survey (OS) maps. Fortunately, 25 of those we bought for JOGLE would be needed on this walk, so only 30 new ones had to be purchased! Once all the maps had been obtained, the next step was to plot the route onto them: mile by mile. This identified where footpaths could be used and where we'd have to resort to roads or cycle paths. After many months of plotting, using all that modern technology provides, such as satellite views of landscapes, and after numerous refinements the route was almost done. The last task was to pre-book all 78 bed and breakfast accommodations needed on the walk, ensuring they were as close to the proposed route as possible. This inevitably caused some further refinements to the route, as accommodation in some places proved impossible to find.

In January 2016, Maureen and I were finally able to agree the route. Every mile was then marked on the maps. I also produced a daily walk profile, by recording the contour height of every mile onto a spreadsheet and using these to create a chart. These would be used on route to remind us each day what lay ahead.

By this time, we'd both retired from work, Maureen in 2012 and me at the end of 2015, so we knew that we'd be free to undertake this challenge in 2016. We'd decided that, just as for JOGLE in 2012, we would start the walk at the beginning of May and finish in July. The month of May is on record as annually being the driest month in Scotland, but it is also vital to be south of the border by June as the dreaded midges invade seemingly everywhere up there for the next 3 months. We love Scotland, but there's no-way we'd ever be there in June, July or August as the midges are just intolerable.

A frequently asked question was whether we'd be looking for sponsorship. A charity dear to our hearts is Thrombosis UK. In August 2011 Maureen's daughter Dawn tragically died of a brain aneurism. She was 30 weeks pregnant at the time with her third child. Baby Molly survived, born by emergency caesarean section. We raised funds in 2012 and decided to do so again, setting a target of £1,041; a pound for every mile.

So often such walks are undertaken by a lone walker, the man who sets off to escape from it all or the woman driven by a worthy cause to attempt a walk she never dreamt she'd take. But on this trip, it's Mr & Mrs Shipley all the way, Martin and Maureen literally hand in hand whenever possible, walking the length of the UK. There will be a great sense of achievement at completing each day's walk together, but it will also bring its challenges and conflicts along the way.

And so, with the May Day Bank Holiday over, the day we'd waited 4 years for was here, the day to leave our home in Derby to embark on this unique adventure. The focus was to get to Scotland in one piece. It's possible to reach our starting base at Durness in one day, but if anything were to go wrong there would be instant pressure to still get there on time. Our starting date was set in stone, not least because we'd pre-booked all our daily accommodation in advance. This worked perfectly on JOGLE, but it meant that we couldn't start the walk late or the whole schedule would be affected.

The plan to get to Scotland was to take a taxi to Birmingham Airport, fly to Inverness, then take a hire car to Durness. Believe it or not, public transport from Inverness to the far north of Scotland only runs on certain days of the week, so a one-way car hire was the only option that would confidently fit into our schedule.

An important activity in planning the journey to Durness was to beg the question 'What If?' What if the taxi hits heavy traffic on the way to the airport and we miss the flight? What if the plane is significantly delayed or cancelled due to modern day issues such as snow in May, security alerts or even an Icelandic volcano erupting, as happened in 2010? What if we arrive in Inverness too late to collect the hire car, or we pick it up okay but are faced with having to drive 250 miles to Durness late at night on unfamiliar, unlit roads?

All too risky for me! So, I planned for us to take two days to get there. The first day we'd travel to Inverness, collect the hire car and have an overnight stay in the town. The next day we'd drive up to Durness with plenty of time in which to do it. After all, a drive through the amazing scenery of north-west Scotland shouldn't be rushed! We'd check-in to our first B&B and then start the walk the following day, all refreshed and rearing to go!

The taxi arrived promptly at 7am. We excitedly threw our holdalls and a couple of carrier bags into the back and jumped inside. Our flight wasn't due until 10.35am, but taking no risks we'd sooner be at the airport very early and spend time there rather than anxiously sitting in a traffic jam. We looked back at our house as we eased down the road, knowing it would be 11 weeks before we'd be back.

We pulled into the drop off point at Birmingham Airport at 8.30am. We made our way through to the airline desks to check-in our holdalls. On our previous trip to Inverness in 2012 prior to walking JOGLE, one of the rucksacks got caught in the baggage conveyor belt at Arrivals and had to be cut free by the ground staff by slicing through the shoulder strap. The rucksack was ruined (instant stress!), but the airport arranged for a replacement to be obtained and delivered it to our hotel. To avoid a repeat of this we'd put our empty rucksacks into old holdalls, along with our gear, and would leave the holdalls somewhere appropriate in Scotland. It was a one-way journey for them!

Thankfully all went well. The flight to Inverness was enjoyable, especially as the visibility through the windows was to ground level. The views of the snow-topped mountains, as we passed over firstly the Lake District and soon afterwards the

Scottish Borders, were fantastic. Footpaths could clearly be seen, and it really got the excitement levels revving up for the big walk.

No problems at Inverness Airport either. With the hire car collected we drove to our hotel on the edge of town, had a pleasant overnight stay and then set off after an early breakfast for Durness. The drive would take us over a good part of our walking route, in so far that we'd be using cycle routes and paths that tracked the A835, and further north we'd be walking on the A894 and A838 roads themselves.

On route, we'd arranged to drop into the B&B at Ullapool that we were due to be staying in at the end of day 6 of our walk. This was to leave a parcel of mainly maps that we'd collect when we reached there. We'd be carrying seven maps at a time on the walk and then we'd need to exchange them for the next seven. To facilitate this our excellent neighbour Brian would post out to us a total of eight parcels on specified dates, with the parcels waiting for us at various prescribed points along the way. On each occasion, we'd post the ones we'd used back home using the same envelope and the prepared address labels and postage stamps that came with it. For our first parcel however, we were acting as Postman Pat since we'd be driving through Ullapool, plus it gave us the comfort factor of knowing our first parcel had arrived!

As we headed for Durness I said to Maureen, "we need to devise a suitable acronym for our walk. We can't keep saying 'Cape Wrath to Dover', we need something snappier". We decided to follow the examples of JOGLE, or as those who walk the more traditional Land's End to John O'Groats version of that walk would call it 'LEJOG'. So, a five-letter acronym was needed. After toying with ideas, we opted for the first three letters of Cape and the last two letters of Dover, resulting in CAPER. It seemed instantly appropriate, as this was certainly going to be 'a bit of a caper!' We got carried away with it after that, imagining that we'd be the Capered Crusaders. People do crazy things on long distance walks. Perhaps we should stop off and buy Batman and Batgirl outfits and walk in those!

A couple of miles south of Durness is the small hamlet of Keoldale. Apart from sitting in a fantastic location overlooking the Kyle of Durness, Keoldale is the starting point for a small ferry that crosses the Kyle to take people to the peninsula on which Cape Wrath is located. After a 5 – 10 minutes crossing, passengers transfer to a minibus which makes a slow and arduous journey of 11 miles over a rough, potholed track out to the Cape Wrath lighthouse. The lighthouse is the starting point for our walk tomorrow, after we've taken this scenic trip. We'd previously experienced the journey in 2013, so when planning this walk I knew what the logistics of getting to the starting point would entail.

As we'd be driving past Keoldale, we decided to drop in just to check out where we'd be parking the hire car in the morning and review the notice boards there for anything we needed to know. One such board had a typed sign saying 'No ferry sailing due to high winds'.

It didn't have a date on it, so we were unsure if it was for that day or for tomorrow. We'd arrived there after the last crossing of the day, so it was impossible to distinguish if there had in fact been any ferries that day.

A very real risk to our walk starting as planned was getting out to the Cape Wrath lighthouse. Whilst it's possible to walk to it, the shortest distance is 11.8 miles up the west coast from Blairmore and then walking the same distance back (total 23.6 miles), or 15 miles from Keoldale, walking south for 2.5 miles to a small bridge over the southern tip of the Kyle, then 2.5 miles back up the other side to the ferry point, to then walk 11 miles to the lighthouse and back (a total 30 miles). For these reasons, we needed to take transport out to our starting point and then walk back 11 miles, a reasonable distance for the first day. In addition to the threat of weather to the ferry crossing the Kyle, the minibus journey goes through MOD designated terrain. If the MOD has decided to have a firing practice day, which they can do at as little as a day's notice, the minibus would not be able to travel.

Our plan was to take the first ferry of the day from Keoldale at 11am, followed by the mini bus ride which takes 40 minutes. We'd aim to start the walk at 12 noon and walk the 11 miles back to the ferry point in time for the last ferry at 4.30pm.

We mused over the intention of the sign as we drove the final short distance to Durness. On the edge of town was our B&B, Aiden House, a seemingly new building of wooden design, with impressive views out to Faraid Head and the north coast of Scotland. Our host, Alexandra, was very welcoming and helpful. We asked if she knew what the weather would be doing tomorrow. "The forecast is for a dry, sunny day, but gale force winds are expected", she said.

This wasn't sounding good. Before looking for somewhere to eat there was one very important call I had to make, to the Keoldale Ferryman. The big question was would the ferry go out in such conditions. In any event Maureen was telling me there was no-way she'd be on it even if it was. In 2013 when we were heading back to the ferry after visiting the lighthouse, the winds had really strengthened. A noticeable swell had developed in the Kyle and it was touch-and-go if the return ferry crossing would happen. We knew it would be rough when the ferryman, who in the morning had been in a tee shirt and shorts, arrived dressed from head to foot in yellow waterproofs like a North Sea trawler man.

I keyed in the ferryman's number and sat with fingers crossed until he answered. John is a lovely guy, who has run the ferry for

38 years. When it comes to whether the ferry will run he's very black and white, it's either a 'yes' or a 'no'. When it comes to guaranteeing a place on the first ferry of the day, which for us was a must, he's the opposite, very non-committal. I'd tried through calls and emails during the planning stage to book a seat on the first ferry, but he has no booking procedure. The ferry takes just 4 people at a time; 'ferry' is a rather grand title for what is a small rowing boat with an outboard motor. What was even more key was booking two of the sixteen places available on the first minibus, but again no booking system. It's a first come, first served scenario, which normally I'd have no truck with, except on this occasion we really couldn't afford to chance it. But I'd not been able to gain any guarantees before we'd travelled, so I'd intended to try again when we got to the area.

"Hi John, this is Martin Shipley. You may remember that my wife Maureen and I are starting a long-distance charity walk from Cape Wrath this week and that we're eager to get on the first ferry and first minibus tomorrow please".

"I'm very sorry", said John, "the ferry won't be going tomorrow due to the forecast gales. Friday, it will definitely go through, 100%".

"OK", I said. "Can you definitely ensure we're on the first ferry and minibus please?"

"Ay, you'll be alright if you're there nice and early", he said.

So, no ferry tomorrow and no firm promise of a couple of places for Friday. 'Damn it', I thought, or words to that effect! Four years of planning and beaten by the weather. I looked in disappointment towards Maureen.

"We need a plan B", I said. "Let's go to the pub and think it through".

8

We freshened up and drove to the recommended Smoo Cove Hotel, a few miles east of Durness. After a very enjoyable pie and chips, which made me feel much better – you can't beat comfort food when you're feeling a bit fed up. I asked Maureen what she thought. "Well, you might not like the sound of this, but I think we should do the day 2 walk tomorrow and hope the ferry goes on Friday as John suggests it will".

"Great idea", I said. "It makes use of the day and will not disrupt our schedule".

As ever, there were some logistics to work through to make it happen, but it did make sense. Fortunately, we had two nights planned in Alexandra's company, so we'd still be coming back to Durness to stop over on Thursday and would then be in the area on Friday and be able to go to Cape Wrath as planned.

Day 2's walk would take us from Keoldale to Rhiconich, a distance of 12 miles. If we walked there the question was how do we get back to Durness? Public transport is non-existent. Taxis are equally rare and may have to come from as far away as Ullapool, costing a fortune. We needed to have a chat with Alexandra.

"You could hitch a ride back with the school bus. You'd have to guarantee to be in place in Rhiconich to be picked up at 2.40pm though", Alexandra said.

Our walking speed, allowing for all eventualities (lie of the land, taking photos, shooting video, toilet stops!) is 2 miles per hour. We'd need 6 hours for the walk, meaning we'd have to set off around 8.00am to be on the safe side. That was doable, but the risk assessor in me was whispering in my head, "what if you're late and miss the bus?"

"What you could do is go with the school bus in the morning and walk back", she said.

"Brilliant, I like it", I said, "how do we arrange it?"

"Leave it with me, I'll make a call and put it in place. All you need to do is be at the bottom of our drive at 7.45am."

We thanked Alexandra and breathed a sigh of relief that we'd still got a day's walking tomorrow, that it would work okay for us and that we'd still be covering our planned route. How crazy was it, though, that having spent four years planning 1,041 miles walk heading due south, that our first day would be spent walking north!

Thursday 5th May 2016 dawned at long last. It sometimes seemed that this day would never arrive, but here it was. We were up early, packed a couple of day rucksacks – no need to take everything we'd got with us – and grabbed a quick breakfast. We were dutifully waiting on time at the bottom of the drive for the school bus, like an eager brother and sister on their first day at a new school. The minibus, as it turned out to be, arrived and I opened the front door. "Slide the side door back and one of you jump in there", said Dave our driver, "and the other is up front with me". I drew the short straw and went in through the side door, where the school kids were waiting, seemingly uninterested in these two oversized pupils getting on board. Then I realised that, like most teenagers, they either had headphones on or were glued to their iPad's. At least Dave was sociable, and we had a good chat as he drove at speed down the road, as if the school bell would be ringing anytime now.

The drive to Rhiconich took just 20 minutes, the walk back would be 6 hours or so! But it served to enable us to view our route for the day, as we'd be walking back using the road. Scotland has few actual footpaths as we'd know them in England and Wales. Those that do exist are not marked in green on OS maps, but are shown as small black dotted lines, generally heading across the country west to east, enabling access to the exciting Munro mountains and the 1,500 lochs. Few paths run north to south, other than cycle routes which we will use in due course. For now, and for the next 100 or so miles, we'd be walking on tarmac. In terms of our route, we'd spend 2/3rds on paths and 1/3rd on roads, but in Scotland the equation reverses to 2/3rds on roads and 1/3rd on paths.

Dave pulled up at the side of the road just inside Rhiconich, before he turned right to head towards the west coast where a day's education awaited our learned passengers at the Kinlochverbie High School. We waved them off and crossed the road to a safer, larger area next to one of the few Police Stations in the north-west of Scotland. In fact, there's only one police officer in the region, according to the locals.

So, this is it, the start of our epic adventure, albeit not quite the start we'd planned. The sun was shining and there were blue skies, with just a few white clouds, but it was cold enough for us to have fleeces, over-jackets and woolly hats on. All togged up, it was time to record the occasion on our video camera. I found a suitable rock on which to lodge it, pressed play, then nipped over to where Maureen was standing with the beautiful Loch Inchard behind her.

Recording done, we set off for what was the return journey to Durness. The planned day 2 walk from Keodale would have been 12 miles, but we had an extra two miles to do to get back to our B&B, so we were already doing extra mileage and we weren't even lost!

The walk profile for today was steadily uphill for 4 miles, downhill for the next 4 miles, then flat for the remainder. During the planning period, I'd produced a profile for all 78 days to be walked, to ensure we knew what to expect each day and that there would be no surprises. It didn't always work out that way!

Once past the 4-mile mark we entered a huge valley that really exposed us to the gale-force wind! Several times we found ourselves virtually running as it pushed us along. What a relief it was not to be walking head on into it; going north was turning out to be advantageous after all. We did meet a poor cyclist going into the head wind, heading for Skye, who had long since given up trying to ride his laden bike, but who was hoping that it would be possible to get back on it once he was out of this valley.

The great expanse of the valley was so impressive. We soon came alongside Loch Tarbhaidh, with dry tussock grass forming its banks and mountains rising from the shore on the far side. Walking on the road was proving to be no issue, as the traffic was very sparse, as it tends to be this far north. We were anticipating a quiet time on the roads for the next 44 miles, until we reached Ullapool on day 6.

We reached the 10 miles point in good time feeling a little weather beaten but really enjoying the walk. It was then that the first sight of the southern end of the Kyle of Durness was gained. As we approached we saw that the tide was out, revealing long stretches of sand and slim strips of water with 'white horses' in abundance thanks to our gale force wind. We wondered if the sands would be okay to walk on and if it was possible to wade through the presumably shallow waters, if needs be. Just a thought in case the ferry didn't bring us back tomorrow. But we soon discounted this, especially with the risk of being caught out by the returning tide.

We then spotted a very small footbridge over the tail end of the estuary. This led to a slim path along the grassy shore, but then another estuary to cross over. The OS map indicated a further footbridge about a mile inland. After crossing this, walkers would return to the shore to walk up and over the upper slopes of the Beinn an Amair hillside, just to reach the peninsula ferry point.

We hoped we wouldn't need to take this route in reverse tomorrow and that instead we'd be able to enjoy a couple of pleasant crossings on the ferry.

The few houses that comprise Keoldale were now visible, nestled on the slopes of the hill behind the ferry point. We looked over to them as we passed, then made a short climb up into Durness. We dropped into the local Spar shop for a few provisions, before making our way back to the B&B.

After we'd freshened up we chatted again with Alexandra. She tipped us off that John the ferryman was in the Smoo Cave Hotel bar most nights and that buying him a drink may ensure, more than anything else, that we'd get on the first ferry! So, having enjoyed our evening meal there yesterday, we drove over in the hire car in the hope of spotting him.

As we ate we surveyed the regulars perched on stools at the bar. When our desserts were brought over I enquired if any of those sat by the bar was in fact John. "Yes, the chap in the green shirt", said the waitress. "He's with his two usual 'shipmates', you'll find them all here virtually every night". "Okay, thanks", I said. "The next time they ask for refills of their drinks would you charge it to me, please?"

It wasn't long before these hardened drinkers were ready for their next pint. The waitress pointed to us as she told John who was doing the honours. John came over. "That's very kind of you", he said. "Do I know you?"

"We've spoken before John, on the phone", I said. "I'm Martin, this is my wife Maureen. We desperately need to be on the first ferry and minibus tomorrow to ensure we get to Cape Wrath at the first opportunity, to start our charity walk. We're walking back from the lighthouse to the ferry to take the crossing back to Keoldale".

"That won't be a problem", said John. "I'll look after you, you'll be on it okay".

"Fantastic", I said. "See you in the morning". Given the amount of beer he'd clearly consumed, I wasn't entirely convinced he'd remember us in the morning!

We woke early and peered out of the bedroom window over to the coast. It was a beautiful morning and, more importantly, there was very little wind. The ferry must be going, as John had promised, I thought. All we had to do now was ensure we were on the first crossing.

We had an early breakfast, our last at Aiden House. We offered Alexandra our two unwanted holdalls, which were in very good condition, which she said she could use. We also had a bag of clothes that we'd travelled up in, that we wanted to leave for recycling, which she said she'd sort out for us. Our ever-helpful host then offered to bring a rucksack down to the ferry around 4.30pm after we'd finished today's walk.

Tonight, we needed to be in Rhiconich, where we were scheduled to be after what should have been day 2. So, Alexandra also arranged for the school bus driver to taxi us down to Rhiconich later. What a star!

We drove down to Keoldale in the hire car, parked up at the ferry and stashed the car keys on the ground against the inside edge of the front wheel on the driver's side, as directed by the hire car company. Two guys from the hire company would enjoy a lovely drive out and back from Inverness to collect it.

It was just 10am when we got out of the car. The first ferry wasn't due to go for another hour. To our surprise there was already a queue of eager tourists waiting on the quayside, perhaps because the ferry hadn't gone for several days apparently. The first excitement and risk to us going ahead was a larger boat moored at the quay that needed to move to enable the smaller ferry boat to come in. The owner was remonstrating his luck, as the boat had a flat battery and there was no way to charge it up or jump start the boat. The things you can't foresee, even with good planning. His colleague drove off at speed for Durness, seemingly to fetch a replacement battery.

In the meanwhile, John had arrived, along with Stuart the minibus driver. I spoke with Stuart first. "Morning", I said, "we're Martin and Maureen and you'll no doubt be aware from your manager, Steve, who I've emailed and spoken to recently, of our need to be on the first minibus out to the lighthouse as we're starting a long-distance charity walk from there".

"Hi", he said, "Steve never mentioned anything to me, but we'll sort it for you" he assured me.

"I'm just a bit worried as there seems to be more than the 16 maximum you can take already here", I said.

"Ay, not to worry, it'll be alright", he said in a not too convincing way. It was then I realised Stuart was one of the other guys at the bar last night. Must have been good stuff, whatever they were drinking.

I walked over to John, who was standing by his boat. "Morning John", I said. "Remember us from last night in the bar?" Didn't look like he did, initially. "We bought you a drink".

"Oh ay, I do", he said.

"We really must be on the first ferry and minibus, John. Stuart doesn't seem to know this, but it's really important".

"You'll be on it, I'll see to it", said John.

Stuart then spoke to the assembled day trippers, "Morning everyone. I'm Stuart. We have a maximum of 16 we can take on the minibus at any one time, so I need to count you out. John will then take you over on the ferry, 4 at a time". With index finger pointed, he started his count from our left. We shuffled forward, anxiously. Deep joy, we were counted in as numbers 7 and 8. There were five tourists that he couldn't include, whose only recourse was to return for the next set of crossings at 1pm.

The obstructing boat had been removed from the quay following a fresh battery being installed. We watched as the first four passengers boarded the ferry and sped across the rich blue water, which was as calm as the proverbial duck pond, and alight at the other side. John was equally swift in returning, a round trip of just under 8 minutes. We clambered on board, eased down onto the wooden slats that served as seats and off we went. The water remained very calm and it was a delightful way to start the day, now that we could relax and enjoy it.

As we travelled John leaned towards us and said, "Don't pay me for the ferry, please put the money towards your fund raising". We thanked him for his generosity and soon we were disembarking on the other side.

"You'll be back in time for the last ferry at 4.30pm, won't you?" he asked.

"Yes, we'll march back to be here by then", we assured him. We knew we'd have to be covering 3 miles per hour, which is a little faster than we usually walk, but heading for the last ferry is like aiming for the last bus somewhere, you don't want to miss it!

After two more boat trips, all sixteen of us were across and ready to go. Stuart fired up the ageing minibus and we were off. A steep climb out from the quayside led to amazing views over the Kyle of Durness, as it flowed out to sea. The 11-mile journey would take 40 minutes, with Stuart explaining that due to the state of the track he was seldom able to use more than second gear. The white bus stood out against the largely brown landscape, which had little wildlife evident and no buildings once we were a mile or so into the journey. The MOD use the area for manoeuvres and firing practice, as the landscape is regarded as being very similar to the Falklands. It's the only area in the UK where they are allowed to use live ammunition, Stuart informed us. Fortunately, there was no MOD activity today, so no dodging bullets on the way back, thankfully!

Like yesterday, the outward journey provided an opportunity to view the route back. There was zero chance of us going wrong, as it's a very clear almost white track against the brown grasses, and the only track that exists. As we dropped over the summit of the final rise of the track on the outbound journey the white lighthouse with its black dome came into view, looking magnificent against the clear blue sky. It looks out over the dramatic coastline and the Atlantic Ocean some 122 metres below. The lighthouse was built in 1828, is 20 metres high and has 81 steps to reach the top. Since March 1998 it has been automated, rather than manned, and is managed from a control centre in Edinburgh!

The tourists clambered out of the bus and began spending their allocated hour in the area to look around, before the minibus's return journey. For us it was backpacks on and time to take photographs to record the official start of our walk. I thanked Stuart and got my cash out to pay him.

"That's okay", he said, "Donate it to the charity, please. We'd welcome a bit of promotion of the ferry and the trip to Cape Wrath on your social media sites, if that's okay".

"Absolutely", I said, "And we're very grateful to you and John for everything".

I felt very emotional now, for after 4 years of planning and organising, worrying and being anxious about all manner of things that could go wrong, we were here at Cape Wrath. Now it was just a matter of walking 1,041 miles over the next 78 days - correction, 1,029 miles over 77 days now after yesterday! - until we reach Dover and its castle.

Photos done, we set off at 12.15pm passing through the two stone pillars that mark the entrance to Cape Wrath and walked up the first short climb of the day, looking back towards the lighthouse as we went. The weather remained glorious and it would continue that way throughout today's walk.

As we dropped over the summit and headed downhill we were suddenly in splendid isolation. Odds were that we'd not see any other walkers today, as those walking a south to north route to the lighthouse usually take the 'Cape Wrath trail' up the west coast. We were heading south-west for the first 9 miles away from the coast, before turning due south to shadow the Kyle estuary. However, by our calculations the minibus would pass us at around 4 miles as it journeyed back, so we should see our fellow travellers at least one more time.

And so, it proved to be. At 4 miles, down the track the minibus pulled up at a viewpoint to allow the tourists to alight and take photos of a distant secluded beach at Kearvaig, the only one along the north coast between the lighthouse and the Kyle estuary. As the passengers got off, several came over to us and gave us donations. Stuart had been telling them why we were not on board, with Valerie, Vic, Lynda, Roger, Gordon and Wendy kindly donating to our fund raising. All passengers climbed back on board and we watched as the minibus soon became a white speck on the distant landscape. We were alone again; the place was ours. A perfect moment for a spot of lunch. I do love it in landscapes when there is no noise, just a huge natural environment where the silence is only occasionally broken by the most natural of sounds, birds, wildlife, the wind and the sea.

The track was hard going underfoot at times, with frequent potholes, so although straightforward, care was needed to ensure no early trips or falls occurred. I always worry about injuries or illness at the start or towards the end of a long walk. Somehow once a few days have been done it becomes less of a conscious thing, whilst always taking care of course.

The 9 miles point was approaching as we reached the turning point to head due south. As we met the Kyle we saw that the tide was now out and, just like yesterday, long swathes of sand were revealed with a thin snake of water heading inland from the sea. With the blue skies, a few white clouds, green grassy hills along the shore and a great expanse of beach, the views were truly magnificent. I probably took more photos and video footage here than at any point on the walk. The final 3 miles to the ferry point were glorious. At one point, we spotted half a dozen seals basking in the sun on a stretch of sand.

Soon we could see that a section of the 'water snake' lay along the route the ferry had taken. No need, therefore, to wait for the tide to come in before John could collect us. The fantastic views had led to us strolling along rather than keeping to the required pace and we calculated that we would miss our 4.30pm finish by at least 10 minutes.

"John will no doubt have his binoculars looking across towards the cliffs and will come over when he sees us", I assured Maureen, who was starting to panic.

We started the descent towards the quayside just as we spotted the ferry leaving the opposite side. The water still looked very calm, thankfully, and John was dressed in the same gear he had worn in the morning...no trawler man outfit this time!

After a pleasant final voyage, we said our goodbyes to John. Waiting for us on the quayside was Alexandra with our other rucksack. She had put a call in to Dave, our 'taxi' driver, when she saw the ferry returning and within a few minutes he was with us too. We waved Alexandra off, thankful for such a wonderful host and great help at the start of our walk.

Dave was clearly not hanging around. He sped down the narrow road, which was quite scary sitting perched up on the front seat. Before we knew it, we were jumping out at Rhiconich Hotel, our base for the night, relieved to have gotten there in one piece.

It had been an exciting first two days, not exactly the ones we'd expected, but then that's best laid plans for you. Still, we were here in Rhiconich at the end of day 2, with 23 miles walked, heading south and enjoying every moment of it.

Chapter 2 – A Wee Walk Across The Highlands

It had been a pleasant stay at the Rhiconich Hotel. We'd eaten there last evening, simply because theirs was the only choice in the village, but it was lovely food which we thoroughly enjoyed. Breakfast too was good, and we eased ourselves out of their reception area soon afterwards in good spirits looking forward to the day's walk. There were 11 miles ahead of us, to be walked entirely on the A894. In fact, of the next 70 miles of walking, just 7 of these would be off-road. To those unfamiliar with the North-West of Scotland this would sound very unappealing. The reality though is that there is very little in the way of traffic until nearing Ullapool, which was still over 50 miles away, so for all intents and purposes it would be like walking on a quiet country lane anywhere in the UK.

As we raised the rucksacks onto our backs, we looked at each other and both bellowed a huge sigh. "Good grief, that's heavy", I said. "Mine too", said Maureen. We'd planned what we'd be carrying each day and had packed our rucksacks at home more than once before we left to test how they felt. They'd felt heavy then, but we knew from previous experience that they would initially, until getting used to it. Somehow, they felt even heavier now. "I think it's because we didn't carry full rucksacks on the first two days", I suggested. "This is the first day of carrying everything we have with us. Let's see how it goes. We might have to discard anything that's not essential if we can't manage them", I said.

You're no-doubt intrigued to know what's in the rucksacks, so here's a summary: -

• Socks – 2 pairs walking, 1 pair sports

• Shorts/Trousers – 1 pair, plus 1 pair over trousers

- Undies – 2 pairs (Maureen - 2 pairs plus 1 extra bra)

- T-shirts – 1 walking t-shirt (Maureen – 2 walking plus 1 vest)

- Base layers – 1 long sleeve, 1 short sleeve, 1 fleece

- Coats – 1 lightweight waterproof, 1 lightweight warm

- Hats – 1 woolly, 1 baseball cap

- Gloves – 1 pair (Maureen 2 pairs)

- Hankies – 2 x cloth hankies

- Specs – 1 x bifocals/reading

- Cameras – 1 video plus charger

- Maps – 6 OS maps

- Diary – 1 notepad and 2 pens

- Mobile phones – 1 mobile plus charger

- Food – 1 packed lunch, 2 x water

- Medical – packet of essentials (plasters, pain relief etc)

- Toiletries – bic shaver, tooth brush, toothpaste, comb, sachets of shampoos, small scissors, pumice stone

- Money – cash for B&B's, cheque book, bank & credit cards

- Keys – house keys

- Travel documents – passports, driving licenses

- Other – rucksack cover, compass, spare laces, foam seat pads

The theory was to wear one set of gear and rotate two others. In this way, we would always have at least one set of dry gear even if the other two are either ready to be washed or damp from having been washed. Hand washing is usually the name of the game, though many B&B's will run a wash through if you ask them, often at no charge.

Despite the apparent weight of our rucksacks, we set off for Scourie. It wasn't long before we came across our first loch and there'd be several others roadside over the course of the day. We were now no more than 1.5 miles from the west coast as the crow files and could often look out to sea between the undulating hills. This was scenic country, with bright yellow gorse bushes everywhere. The rugged, almost volcanic ground either side of the road would be very difficult to walk on, whereas our tarmac 'path' was flat and making progress was easy, albeit with no give in the ground. Before the day was out this would cause a few pains in our shins, but nothing to be concerned about.

We decided to take a break every 3 miles, mostly to take the rucksacks off for a while. The weather was dry but overcast, though a pleasant temperature for walking in. Shortly after our first break we met a fellow walker going north. He was walking the Cape Wrath Trail, an extremely tough wild camping trek from Fort William up the west side of Scotland, but generally inland from the winding coastline in order to keep a relatively straight route to the Cape. The going had been that tough that he'd come further inland to the A894 to give his legs and feet some respite from the pummelling of the hard, tussock strewn ground.

With 6 miles completed the quiet of our tranquil meander between the lochs and hills was disturbed by an ever-growing hum that developed into a grand prix-like roar in a matter of seconds. We stepped onto the safety of the grass verge as eight super charged cars in an array of bright colours appeared round the bend. Amongst them I spotted a Lamborghini, Maserati, Bugatti, Porsche and a couple of Audis as they swept by. In 2015 the North Coast 500 tour was created, a 500 miles circular route starting and finishing in Inverness. This has become increasingly popular not only with car drivers but motor bikers and cyclists, who also came by at some point during the day.

We passed our final stretch of water with the catchy name of Loch a` Bhadaidh Daraich, to enter Scourie around 3pm. It's a small village straddled around the main road, with one hotel, a Spar shop and little else, except that we did pass a fish and chips trailer that we noticed was due to be open from 6.30pm. After freshening up and resting, we checked out the hotel for food but, bizarrely, it was only possible to buy a set 4-course meal at £32 each...we thought not! Instead we made our way to the fish and chips trailer, which was now open and cooking freshly caught haddock. Just the job. Not being able to take food back to our B&B, we looked around for somewhere suitable to eat it. Our luck was in. Just down the road was a bus shelter and it had seats too. We enjoyed a superb local dish in the shelter, looking across Scourie Bay and out to the sea.

After a comfortable night, we went down to breakfast, where we chatted to a couple who were touring the north of Scotland in their electric car. Their challenge today was to get to the next charging point along the north coast before the car ran out of power. Our challenge was to reach Kylesku, 10 miles due south. Not a particularly long day, but one of those necessary for the sake of overnight accommodation. We looked out of the windows towards the village green, where the nearby puddles were illustrating a steady downpour of rain, our first of the walk.

We donned waterproofs and over trousers and set off a little after 10.00am, just as the local trawler men were easing their boats into the bay with their early morning catch. Despite the rain it was quite mild, though with a strong head wind which would last for much of the day's walk. The rain eased off after about an hour, with only occasional light showers thereafter, so we could remove the wet weather gear after 3 miles. The scenery continued its mixture of lochs, yellow gorse and undulating, rocky hills. As we passed the attractive Badcall Bay our road noticeably turned south-east and continued this course for the remainder of the day.

Kylesku sits on the tip of the Assynt peninsula overlooking Loch Glendhu. This joins with Loch Glencoul and together they head for the sea via Loch a` Chairn Bha`in. Hense Kylesku is virtually surrounded by water. Our accommodation for the night was the simplistically named Kylesku Hotel, which sits on the banks of Loch Glendhu. This would be our most expensive stay of the entire route, at £140 for bed and breakfast. We also had no option but to eat in, more of a fine dining experience than pub grub. "Make the most of this stay, Maureen", I said. "Use everything the room has to offer and don't be shy to ask for extras". It was a lovely place and a bit extravagant really for long-distance walkers, but my rationale is that providing our average B&B costs of £75 per night would be met overall, we could justify the occasional expensive stay where it was necessary.

As we entered the dining room that evening we were met by a very unusual sight. The chef specialises in sea food and the dish of the day was langoustines. These were served on what can only be described as a set of gallows, such that 6 to 8 langoustines were impaled on a vertical spike which led to the head of the gallows, where diners slid them off one at a time to devour. Something more traditional and straightforward for dinner for us, I think.

Breakfast was a delight too, taken at a table overlooking the loch, resplendent in the early morning sun. Maureen indulged in fresh blueberries and maple syrup pancakes – and why not! The weather forecast was for a dry day at a respectable 23 degrees: shorts weather.

We set off on our last stretch on the A894, which on reaching Loch Assynt at the 6 miles point would join the A837, heading due south all day. The road remained devoid of traffic and there were sections with good grass verges that we used, which were kinder to our legs and knees than the tarmac. We were now some 10 miles inland from the coast and the surrounding hills had become mountains. The impressive Sa`il Gharbh towers above the landscape to 809 metres, a giant mass of solid rock that seemed to watch our every move for several miles as we passed steadily by.

The weather forecast turned out to be conservative. It was a scorcher, easily 28 degrees or more and with strong winds at times too. We'd taken four bottles of water with us and managed to refill two of them at our lunch stop at Inchnadamph, a quiet hamlet at the east end of Loch Assynt. This was an impressive mass of deep blue water, with a promontory projecting into it on which stands what's left of Ardvreck Castle. The walls that remain comprise of a finger of stone, pointing accusingly at the sky, sufficient to identify it as once having been a three-storey tower house of classic traditional Scottish castle design. From Inchnadamph the loch feeds into the River Lonnan, which our 'new road' diligently followed along the valley for the next 6 miles.

With 3 miles to go, the heat was really taking its toll. Loch Borralan came into view and we knew that half way along its north bank would be our B&B, the intriguingly named Altnacealgach Inn – try saying that after a few whiskies! We were desperate to drop our rucksacks and dive into a refreshing shower by now. "Welcome, come in", said Lesley the owner. "I'm afraid we've had a power cut and there's no electricity. That means everything is off and there's a strong possibility of no evening meals, certainly until the power comes back on", she said.

We ventured to our room, a chalet overlooking the loch which we were sorely tempted to jump into to cool off. We could do nothing until normality returned. An hour or so later Lesley came by to say she had found a way to cook something for guests and to head over to the dining room at 8pm. Around 30 minutes later the power was restored, enabling us at last to get freshened up. Pie and mash was the order of the day, which was very welcome, and afterwards we slept like logs!

We awoke the next morning to see the sun already dancing on the calm loch, glistening like diamonds on the water, as it literally warmed to its task of ensuring two game walkers would end the day with a decent sun tan! A jaunt of 18 miles faced us to the lovely town of Ullapool, which we last visited 6 days ago on our journey north to Cape Wrath.

Shorts, tee-shirts and covered in sun cream – was this really Scotland in May? At breakfast Lesley seemed concerned for us. "Do take plenty of drinking water with you, it's going to be another scorcher out there today", she said. Then came the music to our ears. "I'll be going to Ullapool this morning", she said. "I'll take a rucksack to your next B&B if you wish". I think our instant "yes please, that'll be fantastic" confirmed we did wish! We piled everything into Maureen's rucksack that we didn't need for the day and left it with Lesley as we said our goodbyes.

We had six bottles of waters with us and had started on the first one before we'd completed a mile. Boy was it going to be a hard walk, with little chance of finding shade along the way. Maureen was my main concern, as being fair of skin, she doesn't cope with high temperatures very well, let alone when doing an 18-mile walk.

At 4 miles, just as we were admiring a herd of deer in the grasses on the outskirts of Elphin, a silver car pipped us as it passed and then came to a halt a little way ahead. The driver's door opened and out stepped Lesley. "Are you doing okay", she asked. "So far, though it's very hot", said Maureen. "I've got some more water for you", she said, as she thrust four more chilled bottles towards us. "That's brilliant, thank you, we'll need it", I said. And with that she was off, our rucksack securely in her car boot on its free passage to Ullapool.

After 5 miles of relatively flat terrain, the next 2 miles were uphill. Thankfully at the top there was shade and we decided to take a good break there to recuperate. As we sat on a rocky mound, the views across the volcanic-like landscape were again stunning. In the distance was the unmistakable outline of Stac Pollaidh, at 672 metres not the highest mountain around here, but one that evokes memories of a very rainy day in May 2014 when we walked up it and around the summit. How we'd welcome a drop of the wet stuff today.

We resumed in the knowledge that apart from the odd, short incline the route for the remaining 11 miles was generally downhill. Step by step we were getting there, but it was getting hotter by the hour. With the temperature pushing 30 degrees the welcome sight of Loch Kanaird came into view. A wide expanse of water into which jutted a pier, from which an armada of sailing boats had strutted out to sea and were floating merrily on the shimmering water, taking full advantage of the light breeze. As we left the bay behind the welcome sight of Ullapool came into view. With predominantly white buildings, Ullapool sits proudly on the banks of Loch Broom, which continues for some 6 miles inland. We gained an instant impetus to finish the last 3 miles, but although safely in view it would be another hour or so before we reached the sanctuary from the sun that was our B&B, the Riverside Guest House.

Ullapool looked radiant in the sun, the loch reflecting the blue cloudless sky above it. We could see beyond the town's busy harbour to the distant mountains that remained snow-capped, despite the heat. We turned off the main road, snaked through a couple of side streets and there in front of us was our resting place for the night. In planning the walk, I saw reaching Ullapool as the first significant milestone. It is the first town of any size on the route, with all the usual amenities you'd expect at our disposal, and was the final point of walking due south down the west coast of Scotland. Tomorrow onwards we'd be heading south-east until we reached Inverness. At Ullapool we'd completed 77 miles, so it began to feel like we were making inroads into the 1,041 miles of the overall journey.

It seemed longer than 6 days since we'd first met our host, Charlie, when we dropped in on our way north. "Hello again, Charlie, do you remember us?", I said to him. "Ay I do", he replied, "How's it going?" "So far, so good. Very hot today though. Have you still got the package I left with you, please?" With that he went through to his office and soon returned with my brown envelope, the contents of which were the next 7 OS maps, copies of our B&B list and route outline, plus a return label and stamps for posting home the 6 OS maps we'd just used.

After freshening up and relaxing following our long day, we went to the nearby Seaforth Inn for our evening meal before taking an early night. We coupled this with a bit of a lie in the next morning and a late breakfast, as we'd decided to spend the morning in Ullapool. First stop was the Post Office to send our package home, where the array of postcards displayed was such that, call us old fashioned, we just had to buy 4 or 5 to send to family and friends! This was followed by a visit to the Spar to pick up food for the evening, as we'd need to eat at the B&B.

Whilst Scotland was having its expected dry month, we hadn't anticipated that May would experience such high temperatures. By noon it had again reached 26 degrees.

We collected our gear from the B&B and walked down to the harbour area. It was a picture postcard scene, with fishing boats moored next to the key and plenty of people strolling along the harbour road, while others sat on benches admiring the view as they ate their lunches. It would have been easy to take a seat with them for a while, but although we'd just 9.5 miles to cover today we did need to get a move on now. After rounding the harbour and a short climb out of town, the route soon levelled off as we walked along the road. Traffic was busy to start with, but soon quietened off as we distanced ourselves from the tranquil setting behind us. There were plenty of grass verges to use, so the going was good. Loch Broom was with us for the first 6 miles, affording an undisturbed view back towards Ullapool, reducing in size with every mile. We were already looking forward to our next visit, whenever that may be.

It was just 4.30pm when we reached the Forest Way B&B. It was so hot by then that we went immediately for cool showers. It was a beautiful evening as we later emerged from inside our ground-level room into the garden, where we sat for well over an hour eating the food we'd brought with us. The B&B also boasts a bunkhouse, though any takers had yet to arrive, so Maureen decided to check it out. "It's okay if you're happy to share with up to 16 people. It's one room of bunk beds, a small kitchen and a couple of showers", she said. Not our cup of tea, I'm afraid, and neither for that matter are tents. Give us four walls, an ensuite and a good breakfast any day. Admittedly it is quite a costly way to do such a long walk. We're fortunate to have been able to save the funds to use B&B's throughout the walk, but we really wouldn't want to do it any other way.

The sunny weather continued the next day, though thankfully the temperature was more a conducive 20 degrees. Another day on the A835 might not seem exciting to most walkers and ordinarily it wouldn't be for us, but it was necessary in the ongoing absence of footpaths or cycle tracks. Traffic was still light as we made our way up the gradually ascending road, leaving any last glimpses of Loch Broom behind. After 2 miles, we reached the impressive Corrieshalloch Gorge, a deep tree-shrouded chasm below us, with just the narrow River Droma flowing through the gorge, dropping on its journey south through a series of waterfalls. An information board suggested its 2.6 million years old!

It was while pausing to view this spectacle that a cyclist stopped to exchange pleasantries with us. He was using a traditional drop handlebar racing bike, laden with bags on the wheels in support of his tour around the north west of Scotland. "Have you got plenty to eat and drink?", he enquired. "Yes, plenty of water and a few snacks to get us through the day", I replied. "Here have a few more", he said and promptly thrust into our hands a couple of mini Soreen bars and two chocolate bars, which we later had for lunch. "That's amazingly generous of you", we said. "Enjoy your cycling". And with that he was off downhill, while we had 3 more miles of uphill to contend with.

At 6 miles, the road levelled out and entered the Dirrie More valley. It was absolutely deserted, and you could have heard the proverbial pin drop quite easily. Wonderful scenery was all around us, massive mountains, undoubtedly some of Scotland's famous Munros, some with snow still clinging to their upper slopes. The small but perfectly formed Loch Droma sat adjacent to the road, the crystal-clear water strewn with rocks along its banks. Taking our boots off and having a paddle would have been so good, but we resisted on this occasion. The clear blue sky was dotted with white clouds, but none dense enough to prevent continuous sunshine throughout today's walk. We soon came alongside Loch Glascarnoch, a 4.5 miles expanse of water dominating the valley, at the end of which would be our accommodation for tonight, the Aultguish Inn. This was high, exposed land now, so much so that just before the inn were snow gates that would be used to close the road to traffic when the heavy winter snow fell.

We took a short break to eat our snacks and take the rucksacks off for a while. "My back is really aching", said Maureen. "I don't think I can carry it much further". "Well we can't leave it, so I guess I'll just have to carry it", I said. I don't know where this bravado came from, as it was tough enough carrying my own rucksack. But I'm a pragmatist and the black-and-white position was that there was no alternative. I hoisted Maureen's rucksack up and threw it over my right shoulder. Strangely I didn't feel the extra load hit me as I'd expected and somehow it didn't feel too onerous. I managed to carry it for 3 miles and then Maureen took it for the last mile and a half. I hoped I wouldn't regret it in the morning.

We reached Aultguish Inn around 5pm, freshened up, did some hand washing which we hung outside in the strong breeze, and then ate in the bar. The inn sits alone beside the road, with no other buildings or hamlets for 10 miles in either direction. During route planning, this was one of our "must get in" accommodations. This was also a significant point on our epic trek, having completed 100 miles – only 941 to go!

A good night's rest was followed by a later start as we'd got just 9.5 miles to walk today. Plus, shock horror, the weather had changed, and the sun was having a day off! It was overcast outside and feeling very fresh, so it was back on with full length trousers, warm coat and woolly hat. What a difference a day makes!

After 3.5 miles on the road, we took an opportunity to grab an early hot drink at the Inchbrae Motel. It's almost impossible to know when to expect a cafe or similar place to be on route, so sometimes it's just a case of 'if you see it, use it'. The friendly owner took us through to a table in the large conservatory at the rear of the property. This afforded a nice view over their grounds to the trees and brook beyond. We ordered a couple of hot chocolates and started to look around whilst we waited. I couldn't help but notice a nearby candle in a classic brass candlestick holder, which had clearly been there at much hotter times inside this conservatory. It was originally quite a tall, upright candle, but having succumbed to the heat it was completely bent over, still in its holder, its wick pointing directly to the floor. A severe case of brewer's droop sprang to mind! I was obliged to photograph this and later post it onto Facebook with a suitable caption.

Warmed through by our drinks, we stepped outside again to continue our journey. A respite from the road was just around the corner. In planning this day I'd found a turn off onto a forest track that would give us the next 3.5 miles away from any traffic. The track gained height, enabling great views down and across the heavily wooded valley. Scotland has many, many trees but most of them are plantations, accounting for a thriving forestry industry. The track re-joined the road at 7.5 miles. We crossed over onto a minor road, which passed over Little Garve bridge, to then lead to Garve Train Station. We took the footbridge over the railway line, leaving just a few hundred yards remaining until we reached Birch Cottage B&B, where we were warmly welcomed by Ray and Linda. Their website had mentioned that Ray was a former chef and that he did evening meals, so we took the opportunity to eat in and enjoyed a lovely meal.

It was still early when we'd finished eating. We felt a little restless and in need of a change from our usual nightly routine. Linda advocated the local pub, a short distance down the road, where a renowned piano accordion player was appearing that night. Why not, we thought. We soon got there and noticed three tour coaches as we passed through the car park on our way to the entrance hall. The action was taking place in a large lounge to the rear, which as we entered proved to be pretty much full of people, no doubt mostly from the coaches, seated at tables situated around a central wooden dance floor. We parked ourselves in a back corner on a couple of chairs. The accordion player was ready and launched into his first number. He played a couple more and then it was time for him to get to know his audience. He introduced himself and his accordion career to date and then proceeded to ask each table in turn where they were from. To be honest some of the answers sounded like a foreign language to us, but the first four tables were evidently from different cities in Scotland. Three more tables later and the trend was the same. Progress was being made in our direction. The room was full of natives, friendly ones at that, but we couldn't help but try to sink progressively further into the background, hoping to be ignored. It was to no avail. "And the lovely couple in the corner, where are you from?", he asked. "Derby in England", I said bravely. "Wow, Sassenachs are in the room", he announced. "Fear not, you're more than welcome", he proclaimed. He was actually very good and we stayed a couple of hours rather than the 10 minutes we envisaged.

Next morning, after a great breakfast by chef Ray, we set off for the Muir of Ord, a 14-mile stint. The sun had returned and the temperature soon rose sufficiently to convert trousers into shorts and for our fleeces to come off. The first 6 miles were again on a forestry track, initially overlooking Loch Garve, before heading into an area where most of the trees had recently been felled and logged, then stacked neatly in symmetrical piles like brown coloured cigarettes.

On leaving the track we entered the small hamlet of Contin, where we took a coffee break. We returned to our old friend the

A835 for 2 miles, before turning off down a lane into the village of Marybank. We looked around for somewhere to sit as it was time for a lunch stop, but there were no forms or anywhere suitable to be seen. We then saw that the local primary school had kiddies' benches in the grounds and, as it was a Saturday and no-one was about, we passed through the small, unlocked gate and took up temporary residence.

Today was proving to be one of those unspectacular days that happen now and then. The scenery was pleasant, but nothing special, and the walk was going okay. It was just a case of doing it for the cause! We reached Muir of Ord around 4.30pm and soon found our B&B, a modern two storey triangular shaped house, where internally polished wood was everywhere. It was also festooned with a collection of model shire horses pulling whisky wagons, a reflection of the owner having worked in the local whisky distillery most of his working life. There are 98 such distilleries in Scotland, employing around 10,000 people and generating some £4.3 billion from exports alone. The most memorable part of the day was when we went to eat at the nearby Ord Arms, where we had the most wonderful venison!

The next morning as we got ourselves ready for the day, I contemplated the walk ahead. In terms of making progress south we would barely achieve 3 miles. Our 11 miles would largely be due east, but it was nevertheless one we were looking forward to. We'd be returning to Inverness, a town we really like, and which has been pivotal to a number of our previous visits to Scotland. It seemed longer that 12 days since we were last there, following our flight from Birmingham.

The temperature had returned to normal and it was a cloudy, overcast type of day. After 2.5 miles of pavement walking we turned right onto Shore Road. As its name implies the road ran alongside the shore of Beauly Firth, a major inlet from the North

Sea via the Moray Firth. It was a quiet area, virtually traffic free, enabling a chorus of birds to be heard as we walked, along with the lapping of the water on the occasional stretches of sand. We soon reached the small village of Milton, just as a passing shower caused the wet weather gear to be donned temporarily. The views across the Firth were delightful, with towering mountains in the distance, whilst in the foreground rape seed fields added a shocking yellow to the landscape. Patches of trees lined the road, with a carpet of blue bells hiding in their shade. With the rain short lived and the sun soon breaking through, the miles to the adjacent hamlets of Charleston and then North Kessock could only be enjoyed and savoured. This was an ideal place for a spot of lunch, the sun now shining on the blue water as we sat on a handily provided bench outside the local Spar shop.

Suitably refreshed we braced ourselves for the steep climb up a long flight of steps from the shore and onto Kessock Bridge. The transition from waterside tranquillity to thunderous traffic noise hit us like one of the many trucks going over the bridge, though not literally of course! Once over the Firth we took a cycle path down to a minor road that would take us into Inverness. On route, we passed a depot where newly manufactured wind turbines were stacked ready for shipment to their planned windy locations. We've often seen these immense structures whilst on walks, but never this close. They were huge. The last mile was along the banks of the River Ness, a fast-flowing river seemingly in a never-ending rush to reach its namesake Loch Ness, 6 miles or so downstream.

Soon we reached our riverside Premier Inn accommodation and checked in. Later, from our table in the restaurant, we looked out over the river, its bridge illuminated at night together with many buildings along both banks, providing a pleasant outlook as we ate our evening meal.

Our wee walk across the Highlands, from the west coast at Ullapool to the east coast at Inverness, was completed. We'd be in this vast region for another 5 days yet, but our route would now head due south and enter the amazing Cairngorms.

Chapter 3 – Not A Care In The Cairngorms

Inverness gave us the opportunity to stock up on a few essentials, especially sun protection cream, though an overcast day was forecast for today.

We crossed the Ness Bridge over the river (are all things water related called Ness around here?) and walked along the embankment below Inverness Castle. The current red sandstone castle was built in 1836, though there have been a series of castles built and subsequently destroyed on the site since the 11th century.

Our early goal was the Old Edinburgh Road, which we soon turned into, rising steeply from the riverside to head out of the town centre. We followed this for 2 miles until joining General Wade's Military Road. Now, here was a man we'd be very appreciative of before we crossed the border into England. On 10 May 1725 George Wade was appointed by King George 1st Commander in Chief of His Majesty's forces, castles, forts and barracks in North Britain. Over the next twelve years he directed the construction of some 240 miles of roads, plus 30 bridges. Nowadays his roads are tracks that are still very much evident on OS maps and which during planning I'd made every possible use of. This first encounter was a steep climb until we reached our 4 miles point, where it levelled off. This was a great vantage point, from where we looked back towards Inverness and the mountains beyond.

The path snaked through a sparse wood before dropping down to cross Faille Bridge spanning the River Nairn. Whilst this was pleasant, albeit unspectacular scenery, it was nevertheless great to be walking off road, as the path passed by a quarry to enter forestry plantations which surrounded us until we reached the hamlet of Moy. Here another first, as after crossing the busy A9 road we joined the cycle track that runs beside it, the start of a long association!

The cycle track became a minor road before running into the small town of Tomatin, our destination for today's 15-mile walk. It was so small, in fact, that there wasn't any accommodation or eating places to be found there. Instead I'd booked us into Glenan Lodge, situated a mile or so before the town and located next to the Tomatin Distillery.

A benefit of modern technology is that at most places we stayed there was free Wi-Fi. Evenings in remote B&B's are not so isolating as they once were, being able to catch up on emails and texts, and make a daily contribution to the Country Walking Facebook Group. We had some excellent messages of encouragement and by this point some 1,000 people were following our progress. I also took the opportunity to access eBay to bid for a London Marathon 1993 medal for Maureen, who had completed the event but no-longer had her medal. The things you can do in a B&B that you wouldn't be able to do camped in a tent in the middle of nowhere!

The next morning, we awoke with some excitement. Today we'd be reaching the Cairngorms National Park, a dramatic mountainous area of breath-taking scenery. We're no strangers to the area, having walked and toured in and around Aviemore. We've been up the CairnGorm Mountain itself more than once and ridden on the exciting funicular railway to its summit. Aviemore was two days away yet. Today we were off to Carrbridge, hoping for 10 miles of enjoyable walking.

After an enjoyable breakfast, we set off around 9.30am, initially walking through the grounds of the nearby distillery, which has been brewing whisky since 1897. A quiet lane led into Tomatin, the kind of place that if you blink you'd miss it, hence we were soon through and out the other side. At 3.5 miles, we came to a sign proclaiming Slochd Summit, where our lane joined the A9 and the cycle track reappeared. One of General Wade's Military Roads came to this point too, as did the rail line. The significance of the Slochd Summit was its height of 401 metres, making it the second highest point for roads and rail lines between Inverness and Perth.

A little further along we passed another large sign, this one announcing that we were indeed entering the Cairngorms National Park. Our cycle path veered off to the right here and headed into a forestry area. With many trees having been felled, great views opened and being away from the road meant it was now very peaceful and quiet. We were just enjoying the tranquillity when suddenly we heard "beep-beep". My mobile phone had picked up a signal from out of the ether and a new email informed me that my medal bid on eBay had been successful!

We reached Carrbridge relatively early, so we dropped into a cafe for a snack, followed by a visit to the local Spar. Our accommodation, the Craigellachie Guest House, was just along the main road. The door was opened by the owner, James, who beckoned us into the hallway out of the light rain that was now falling. After a day's walk, we usually just wanted to get to our room, get out of our walking gear and freshen up. Whilst we appreciate not everyone stays in B&B's as regularly as we do, sometimes an owner will treat guests like they've never stayed anywhere before in their lives. James was in this mould, taking a full 30 minutes to cover everything about the place and its contents, how to work the shower and even demonstrating how the wardrobe doors open and close! We did try to intervene a few times with a "yes, that's fine, thank you", but our hints were overlooked.

Similarly, in a morning we like to dive into the cereals and coffee and have a light cooked breakfast, then set off on our walk. James, however, had a routine and proceeded to take us through everything on the menu and then be very particular about serving things in whatever he deemed to be the right order, very spaced out time-wise. His intentions were honourable, but if all 78 B&B's on our walk operated like this it would feel like it was taking an extra week to complete it!

So, somewhat later than anticipated, we set off on day 14 for our 10 miles walk to Aviemore. It felt great that we'd now completed the first two weeks of our journey, having walked 159 miles and both of us being in good physical condition. No arguments or even disagreements so far either...inevitably it won't last, but we'll cross that proverbial bridge when we get to it.

Speaking of bridges, we soon passed the Old Packhorse Bridge in the centre of the village, which spans the River Dulnain. No longer in public use, it was originally built in 1717 as a means of enabling funeral processions to access Duthil Church when the river was flooded. Because of this, it was known locally as 'the coffin bridge'. All that remains of the bridge is a single span, arcing high into the air across the rushing river below.

The weather honeymoon was over. Our 2 weeks in the sun had now turned into heavy rain, but the temperature was still reasonable, so we kept shorts on under our over trousers.

The first 3 miles were spent in natural woods, as opposed to plantations, culminating in the first 'cow moment' of our Caper. In fact, there were about 100 cows gathered by the field gate some 25 metres ahead, exactly where our path was leading us. Instant avoidance action was taken, by climbing a gate into an adjacent field, then over another gate into a second field, by-passing the cows from this haven and then returning via stiles to our route.

Our bovine experience was a reasonable excuse shortly afterwards to drop into the first café in Boat of Garten, and to get out of the rain. When we emerged, the rain had virtually stopped. We were now in an area called Strathspey, the River Spey nestled in the valley at the far end of town. Here we joined the Speyside Way, one of Scotland's' four "long distance routes", what are otherwise called National Trails in England and Wales. The route's way markers depict a thistle, the national emblem and national flower of Scotland.

It was a pleasant if uneventful last 5 miles to Aviemore, shadowing the rail line of the Strathspey Steam and Vintage Diesel Railway. No trains running today though. With the skiing season over and the summer season yet to get truly underway, the town seemed quiet as we walked down the high street to find our accommodation for the night.

Next morning, with no need to pick up supplies, we got straight into the day's walk, a 16-mile stint to Kingussie. After taking a left off the high street to reach the hamlet of Inverdruie, we soon turned right onto the B970 and a return to road walking. Although I'd planned 2 or 3 stages off this road, it proved so quiet and so good for making progress that we stayed with it all the way to Kingussie.

Our route continued to track the River Spey in a south-westerly direction. After 8 miles, the river flowed into Loch Insh and out the other end. We could see glimpses of the CairnGorm mountain range to the east through the inevitable forestation, with a more open aspect to the west across a flat and wide green valley, beyond which steep sided mountains reached up to touch the low hanging clouds.

As we turned a corner with just a few miles remaining we were confronted by the impressive sight of the Remains of Ruthven Barracks. They sit proudly on top of an old castle mound and cover a significant area of land. Although destroyed in 1746, the remains of the barracks consist of walls three storey's high, with a series of open windows, probably used to fire down onto an invading army. There is also a separate large barn-style building, also made of stone. Overall some 120 soldiers would have been based at the barracks when it was operative.

Whilst we would have liked to look around this impressive piece of history, it had been a long day and so headed straight for town, to find the Allt Gynack B&B, where we enjoyed a very comfortable overnight stay.

There was a light drizzle of rain as we set off the next morning for Dalwhinnie. Another long day of 17 miles lay ahead of us. The first challenge was to get to the A9, which strangely necessitated us climbing over a decently high wire fence. If there was an easier way to achieve this goal we didn't spot it! Just a few hundred yards along the grass verge were needed before we turned off onto another of our great friend General Wade's Military Roads.

The 7 miles along this track to Etteridge were very scenic and quiet. The track undulated across ground hugging gorse, with an open landscape of modest hills and a gently flowing stream. We took a short break by a small bridge arched over the stream, a quiet secluded location and a sunny interval appearing just at the right time. Soon afterwards we passed the three properties that comprise Etteridge before crossing back over the A9 to pick up the cycle path, a quiet back-road leading to Dalwhinnie. From here it was heads down for the last 4 miles to seek out our B&B for the night, Balsporran Lodge. What a wonderful name for a Scottish B&B!

Balsporran Lodge is located within the Drumochter Pass close to the River Truim. It sits in the shadows of three huge Munro mountains, the A' Mharconaich, Beinn Udlamain and Sgairneach

Mhor, all of them in excess of 900 metres high. It is very isolated and the only accommodation in the area. The white building stands out from quite a distance away, making it easy to spot. We turned off the cycle track down a long footpath, with the lodge situated at the far end, well back from the A9 road. It does though have a railway line running quite close behind it. As we approached I remembered reading that the lodge comprises of three terraced houses joined together as one. Surprisingly all 3 front doors remained, with no clear indication of which was the one to use. We plumped for the middle one and struck lucky.

Phil and Ann both answered the door and gave us a warm welcome. We could instantly see that this B&B had character, not least in the amazing staircase. A dividing wall had at some point been removed, but the two staircases either side of it were left in place, resulting in a very wide sweeping stairway leading to the upper level. By contrast, at the east end of the property, incorporating the lounge, dining room and kitchen and rooms above which our hosts lived in, they'd put in a spiral staircase, so they could quickly move between levels rather than trekking to the central stairs.

After freshening up we went down for our evening meal and enjoyed Ann's wonderful venison. Back in our room we were just reflecting on a lovely day and having reached the 200 miles point, when the first train came by. Evidently, we were near enough to the track for the room to vibrate and one or two of the ornaments to tinkle to the rhythm of the passing carriages. There was only one other train that evening at 10pm, so the potentially disturbed night's sleep didn't materialise – either that or we were too tired to have heard any others!

Our breakfast table the next morning was shared with two very friendly guys from Holland who were touring in the Cairngorms. Of course, they spoke very good English and we could exchange experiences and what we were all doing. As one of them was coating his full Scottish breakfast with brown H.P. sauce, I couldn't resist asking him if he knew where it was made. "In London?" he suggested. "No, actually it's in the Netherlands", I said, upon which they both inspected the label to determine where in their homeland such a classic UK product was being manufactured. It was nowhere I'd heard of!

If the sunny weather honeymoon had been over for the last 2 days, this morning I think the sun had cleared off and filed for divorce. It was bucketing down with rain and judging by the water running past the lodge it had been doing so throughout the night. We donned our waterproofs, bade farewell to one and all, and stepped gallantly out of the front door. At least we'd be on solid ground using cycle route 7 all the way to our destination of Calvine, 15 miles due south.

For the first 2 hours, it was a case of heads down and getting a good march on, as the wind and rain combined to make it seem like we were walking in a power shower. The nearby mountains were all but lost in the accompanying mist and for all intents and purposes the rain looked set in for the day as it continued unabated. A sign announced that we were entering Perth & Kinross 'the heart of Scotland' as we continued through the Drumochter Pass, a huge sweeping valley with the River Truim and the rail line to our right running the length of the valley bottom. It was flanked by moorland on both sides and overshadowed by yet more dramatic mountains. The rain and mist gave it a grim and sinister appearance, with severe weather conditions undoubtedly experienced here in winter. As we reached Drumochter Summit a sign informed us that this is also the highest point on the British railway network, at 462m.

Around midday the weather suddenly changed. The rain stopped and apart from a few short drizzles it stayed largely dry for the rest of the day. The sun must have decided divorce was a bit extreme and chose instead to return and show its face again, peering out behind the clouds occasionally, seeking a reconciliation.

We looked for somewhere dry to stop to eat our packed lunches and came across an unusual bench. The seat and back rest comprised of six old skis, attached to a wooden 'L' shaped frame. For reasons best known to those who erected it, there was also a colourful totem pole with a weird bird's face at the top, sporting two large white eyes, below that a mouse emerging from a hole, then a bear's head and finally a ram! As we sat on the bench Maureen said that her boots had let in water when the rain was at its height. She pulled both boots off to find that her socks were soaked. The boots were new just before we started the walk, so this was disappointing.

"What am I going to do now?" she said, "I can't walk in wet boots".

"Best thing is to change to dry socks and when we get to Calvine we'll take a good look at them", I said.

Having finished our sandwiches, Maureen donned fresh socks and we set off on the final stretch of today's walk. Maureen's boots were so wet on the inside that she had to use a third pair of socks before we reached Calvine. The cycle path made for easy walking though, on what was the original A9 road. Although the OS map depicts it as immediately next to the current A9, which technically it is, the unexpected bonus was that it is some 25 metres lower and separated by a tree inhabited bank, meaning the busy traffic could barely be heard.

By the time we reached our accommodation, the Struan Inn, the sunshine was back in all its glory. We hoped the reconciliation would last into tomorrow and beyond! Once in our room we inspected Maureen's boots. There was a split in the seams on both boots where each foot bends and there was no-way they were going to last the journey. "I'll put a call in to Cotswold Outdoors", Maureen said. We'd bought the boots at the Nottingham Branch of our favourite gear supplier, where we are regular visitors, in early Spring. The appropriately named manager, Alan Walker, runs a great store that gives excellent advice and support, seldom encountered these days. Maureen told him of the predicament.

"Not a problem", Alan said, "We'll get a replacement pair out to you. Where do you want them sending to?" Maureen opted for Kirkcaldy as the next significant place we'd come to.

"Brilliant, many thanks Alan", said Maureen.

After freshening up we parked ourselves in the residents' lounge prior to dinner and it was then that we saw our one and only red squirrel during our time in Scotland. It attacked the wire cage of the bird feeder in the garden with admirable determination trying to get at the nuts inside. It soon gave up and left, but it was great to see it so close.

The sun was up before we were the next morning, with the promise of a much better day ahead for our walk to Pitlochry. We felt surprisingly relaxed today, as if we hadn't a care in the world, as we walked the final few miles within the Cairngorms National Park.

Blair Athol was reached after a couple of hours walking. It's a small town with the impressive white coloured Blair Castle on the outskirts and the customary whisky distillery nearby. As we turned a corner the strong aroma of coffee emanating from the cafe at the Water Mill, a working water mill producing flour and oat meal, proved too much of a temptation and we meekly succumbed to taking a break there.

The surrounding scenery was lovely as we continued, the magnificent Grampian Mountains standing guard over the valley as we reached Killiecrankie. The cycle path became a minor road here, with little in the way of traffic as we followed it until our entry into Pitlochry. Almost instantly we found ourselves in a popular tourist destination, with the pavements to our accommodation a hive of activity. The entrance to Rosehill B&B was tucked away down a short but broad passageway just off the high street, leading to a patio with outdoor tables and chairs. We were greeted there by the bubbly Jackie, who instantly made us feel welcome and comfortable after our 11.5 miles walk. We now needed to rest up as the next four days were destined to be much tougher going.

Chapter 4 – Forth To The Bridge

It was a Monday morning, the start of our third full week in Scotland, as we struggled to raise our heads from the pillows. Like Mondays when I was working, psychologically it can be more difficult to get out of bed, simply because you know the day is called Monday.

Maybe having completed 228 miles since we left Cape Wrath was having something to do with it, but it was all a bit of an effort today for both of us. Before long, however, our routine was in full swing. Showered, dressed and rucksacks prepared, we were soon ready for breakfast. There was also an extra reason to be excited today. Anne from the Country Walking Facebook Group had contacted us a couple of days ago. She lives close to Pitlochry and was keen to meet with us, having been avidly following our progress down the country. But in addition, Anne had offered to do a baggage run for us. Maureen had spoken with her by mobile when she first made contact.

"I can take some of your luggage on to your next stop for you, if you wish?" she'd said.

"That would be fantastic, Anne, and save us carrying stuff we won't be using during the day", said Maureen. "It'll also give my aching back a rest day"

So, it had clearly been decided whose rucksack would be getting a free ride to Dunkeld! That was fair enough as Maureen has osteoporosis and some days her back is painful by the end of the walk.

"I can come to your B&B in Pitlochry on Monday around breakfast time", Anne said. "I can't do Sunday as I've five services to deliver". Anne, bless her, is a vicar.

"Excellent", said Maureen, "Let's say 8.30am. We look forward to meeting you on Monday".

This was a brilliant surprise. The power of social media strikes again. Someone we don't know, whom we've never met, has nevertheless been sufficiently inspired by what we're doing to want to help, and is giving up their valuable time and resources to collect a rucksack and deliver it 14 miles away to Dunkeld, where it will be waiting for us at our B&B when we arrive. All we had to do was make sure someone would be at the B&B to receive it. So last evening when I put in my usual call to the next day's B&B I cleared this with the proprietor. I always check that B&B's know to expect us, despite having ensured I had 78 booking confirmations prior to leaving Derby. An experience of turning up only to find our B&B closed has brought about this worthwhile checking procedure. We put everything that we would need for the day into my rucksack, and then prised everything else into Maureen's, ready for Anne to collect.

We descended the narrow staircase, placed the rucksack for Anne in the hallway and went into the breakfast room, where our host placed us at a table set for four people. Just as we were orienting ourselves with where everything was, two guys who we'd briefly crossed paths with yesterday evening, when we were heading back to our room after dinner, arrived for breakfast.

"May we join you?", asked the first guy.

"Yes, please do", we said in harmony.

Judging by their accents they were clearly Scots, probably in their early forties and seemingly together, if you get my drift. They introduced themselves as Colin and Donald. Colin was the taller of them, standing around 6 feet and being circa 16 stones, I'd guess. Donald was shorter by about 6 inches and would struggle to make 10 stones wet through. What was noticeable about both was that they were wearing quite loud, short sleeve tops, beach shorts and flip flops.

"You both look very summery", I said.

"Ay", said Colin, "we've just come back from Tenerife and thought we'd have a few days in Pitlochry before heading back to Edinburgh. I've a hairdressing business there, Donald's a male nurse. Are you guys on holiday?" he asked.

We told him of our adventure and where we were heading for and generally chatted, as you do, over breakfast together. They were very sociable, and it was a pleasure to get to know them for a while.

"We'll have to make a move", I said, "we've got a friend coming to meet us in a few minutes. I've just got to ask one question before we do though – Donald, where's your troosers?"

Donald laughed. "Ay, I get that a lot. We're still in holiday mood", he said.

Just as we rose from the table we were advised that Anne had arrived and was waiting in the hallway. We eagerly went to meet her.

Anne was a delightful lady, probably of a similar age to ourselves, very positive and bubbly.

"Great to meet you at last", she said. "I've been following your progress down from Cape Wrath. I wanted to do something to support you and thought a baggage transfer might be useful".

"Absolutely and thank you so much for taking the time out of your day to do this for us", I said.

We chatted for about 10 minutes, mostly about walking and the Facebook site, before posing for photographs of the three of us together. We said our goodbyes and then she was gone. It was quite strange, really, to meet a total stranger, willingly hand over half of our on-the-road possessions and then wish her and them bon voyage. In the troubled world in which we live in these days, it's refreshing to know there are kind hearted people out there still who put themselves out to help someone they meet by chance. We wouldn't see Anne again on this trip, but hopefully one day we can return the favour in some way.

Without further ado, it was time to get moving. Today we'd be following cycle route 77, which makes use of minor lanes and 'B' roads. This helps a great deal during route planning, as I could literally travel down the route using Google's street view system. The weather continued to be sunny and warm, as it had been for much of our time in Scotland so far, with temperatures in the mid-20's.

We walked through the town centre to reach a riverside path and then cross the River Tay using a traditional suspension bridge. The sun was already dancing on the deep blue water. We crossed the main road and turned onto the cycle route lane, which would run parallel to the nearby A9, just far enough away for the traffic noise to be a quiet hum. We looked back towards the town to see for the first time the dramatic Grampian Mountains rising high behind it. On the east side of town, the pointed turrets of what looked like a castle towered above the surrounding trees. It was in fact the Atholl Palace Hotel and Spa. It looked magnificent, even from a distance. Maybe we'll come back one day and pay it a visit.

The scenery ahead of us was equally impressive, nice gentle hills and fields, with plenty of trees evident as usual, several arching over our lane displaying their rich, red leaves. If there's one thing Scotland doesn't lack its trees. Wildflowers in the verges were also plentiful. There was an abundance of bluebells and white bells but, uniquely to Scotland we think, there were also pink bells. Often all three colours are in the same patch of ground, the blue ones greatly outnumbering their peers.

At the small hamlet of Logierait we took a short break from the sun by sitting in the shade on bench seats outside the similarly named Logierait Inn. The surrounding area will have looked a lot different when the inn was established in 1710. It wasn't open today unfortunately, so we had to be content with our own drinks. We crossed the River Tay via the delightful white coloured Logierait Bridge, the only community-owned ex-railway bridge in the country. We'd continue to track the river as it flowed south towards our destination of Dunkeld. Lunch was taken at the 10 miles point, at a scenic spot by the roadside.

Soon after resuming our walk we rounded a bend in the lane to be confronted with a large yellow road sign stating, "Road Closed, 24th & 25th May 09.30am to 15.30pm". We sighed with relief, for the closure would start tomorrow. If our progress had been blocked, this would have been where our OS map would come into its own and where a GPS, in my view, fails. The ability to see the bigger picture when you're forced to make a detour is only possible with a large, traditional paper map. All hail to Ordnance Survey Explorer maps!

With three miles to go the 'B' road met up with the noisy A9. We had to turn left and head north for a quarter of a mile to then turn left again and loop down and under the main road to reach a riverside path on the opposite side of the Tay. This would take us through an array of natural trees, resplendent in their spring colours, as it weaved a quiet back way into the north side of Dunkeld.

Just before leaving the riverside we observed a man fly fishing, a popular sport in Scotland. It always strikes me as strange how such fishermen wade out until they're thigh deep in water and then cast out to the far side of the river. Surely, they'd be better just to fish from the other side. They could then drop a decent sized net into the water and scoop the fish up! I also suspect that, unbeknown to the angler, the canny fish are swimming around his ankles to avoid being caught.

Before locating our B&B we treated ourselves to coffee and scones in a local cafe, a suitable reward for completing 14 miles on a hot day. Then it was down the main street to find 'The Bridge' B&B, which would be at number ten. We struggled to find it at first, before spotting that it was indeed a 'number 10', just a door onto the main road not unlike its 'numbers-sake' in Downing Street. All that was downstairs was the entrance hall, with the bedrooms and dining room on the first floor and above. It's so interesting the variety and styles of B&B's we encountered on this walk. And of course, it's the owners that make or break it. We've learnt to realise and appreciate the impact the moment when they first open the door to greet us adds to our impression of the place and determines to a large extent whether we're going to enjoy staying there or not, even if it is for just one night. Barbara was very bright and welcoming – we'd like it here, if everything else was ok!

After a good night's sleep and a fine breakfast, we set off on one of our longer days, but one we were looking forward to, as today we would reach Perth. There were 17 miles ahead of us. The cooler and overcast start to the day was therefore welcome, but it was still warm enough to wear shorts.

We were again following cycle route 77 quite extensively, on hopefully quiet lanes. First task was to re-cross the River Tay to Little Dunkeld, which strangely looks a more populated area on the OS map than its big brother. Surprisingly the scenery for the first 10 miles was very ordinary and unspectacular, just plenty of flat, grassy fields and no hills. It was a case of just doing it today to get the miles done and reach our destination in one piece. I expect days like this occasionally on such a long walk. The UK is brilliant, and we have a lot of fantastic countryside to admire and be proud of, but not everywhere is going to be spectacular.

Such days do though give us the opportunity to regress into what is happening in the real world, that those not cocooned in an idyllic walking bubble are embroiled in. Hot topic at that moment was the forthcoming UK European Union Referendum scheduled for 23rd June, now less than a month away. Opinions were very divided on how to vote, with most people, it seemed, uncertain if they'd vote to 'remain' or 'leave' the EU, these being the two keywords for voters. The few posters that we'd spotted in Scotland were promoting the 'Leave' campaign. Did that indicate a preference in Scotland for voting to exit the EU, or was the 'Remain' view strongest up here and the 'leave' supporters were having to do the greater degree of campaigning? We'd soon find out.

As we'd be on the road on voting day, we'd organised postal votes. The necessary forms weren't due for release by Derby City Council until 1st June, so we'd arranged for ours to be sent to our B&B in Keswick in the Lake District, where we'd be arriving on the 7th. We'd make our individual decisions and pop the completed ballot forms into the post on the morning of the 8th, in plenty of time to be counted in. You never know, our two votes may prove vital to the overall result!

The scenery improved after lunch, with some delightful green rolling hills around us, and with the sun now shining the day literally brightened up. At 12 miles, we reached Almondbank, where we took a coffee break outside the local Spar shop, before locating the path to join up with the River Almond. It was good to get off tarmac, which does take it out of your legs on longer days, particularly as it has no 'give' in it. The softer riverside path was still cycle route 77 and, as we were now nearing Perth and the working day for many was coming to an end, a steady stream of cyclists was accompanying us. The Almond feeds into the Tay, which flows through the city, with the bustling shopping area on its west bank and most of the residential areas over to the east.

Our last mile before reaching Perth Bridge took us alongside the North Inch golf course, in sight of the impressive Balhousie Castle. But we soon swapped the tranquillity of the riverside for the bulging city streets in Perth's rush hour, crammed with noisy traffic. It came as quite a shock, for this was our first city since leaving Inverness 9 days ago. Just as we were dodging between a commuter packed bus and an articulated lorry to cross the main road, my mobile rang. It was our friend Rupert, but I let it go to voicemail as there was far too much traffic noise to even contemplate trying to answer it.

Our B&B, Beechgrove Guest House, was located just along the Dundee Road. A large Victorian house, with landscaped gardens, it looked very inviting. The all-important greeting gained a tick in the box. Anne gave us a warm welcome and a quick introduction to her home. She ended by saying, "...and after you've freshened up feel free to take a wee dram in the dining room". Her offer sort of went over us, for after a tiring day all we wanted to do was get to our room, get our walking gear off, grab a coffee and a shower, and relax for a while. We imagined it was just a colloquialism she uses for the tourists.

Sitting at the window seat with my legs resting up on a chair, I grabbed my mobile to return Rupert's call. We'd met Rupert for the first time in July 2015 when we joined 12 other walkers in Chamonix, France, to undertake a guided Tour of Mont Blanc. Rupert was our guide for this 13 days, 98-mile hike round the Mont Blanc massif, often at heights of 3,000 – 4,000 metres, passing through Switzerland, Italy and back into France. It was a memorable walk and Rupert was a truly brilliant guide. All the walkers became good friends over the tour and email addresses were exchanged before we left, including Rupert's. We'd talked to him about our next adventure in 2016 and he said if he was at all able to he'd like to join us for a day's walking. We'd corresponded before we started and knew he wouldn't be able to walk with us, but he would be in the region and would look to link up somehow.

"Hi Rupert, thanks for calling, how are you?", I asked.

"I'm great, thanks, how are you and Maureen doing?" he replied.

"So far, so good, all going well, 260 miles completed to date", I said. "Are you able to meet up with us?"

He explained that he could, that he'd be travelling down from the north of Scotland tomorrow, where he'd just finished a training course, and was heading for Portsmouth to catch a ferry to Spain for his next guiding assignment. After some discussion about timings, we agreed to meet at 1.30pm tomorrow at a place called the Green of Invermay, 7.5 miles south-west of Perth.

"Great, I'm really looking forward to seeing you both again", he said. "I'll do lunch for you, so don't pack any food tomorrow".

"We'll look forward to that and hearing what you've been up to on your travels, Rupert", I said.

Suitably refreshed, we descended the elegant staircase down to the ground floor to go out for dinner. Before heading for the door, we had a look in the dining room. There sitting regally on top of an ornate sideboard, in a recessed window bay, was a cut-glass decanter and 6 glasses, with a small notice inviting guests to help themselves to a drop of whisky! There were free drams on offer after all, in Scotland of all places!

We rose the next day to more glorious sunshine and another warm day in prospect. We decided to take advantage of being in a city to stock up on some basic items, especially sunscreen which we were getting through as if we were holidaying on a Mediterranean island in the height of summer.

When designing this walk, finding a route out of Perth was one of the more difficult and time-consuming tasks. Our target for today was a small village called Glenfarg, around 9 miles due south as the crow flies, but the problem was how to get past a spaghetti junction lookalike on the M90, the Criagend Interchange. Also, once out of Perth there are no bridges across the River Tay, so heading east of the junction is not an option. There are no quiet paths or lanes on the west side of the motorway that head due south, but there is a minor road that goes under it heading south-west. The issue then was how to get across a tributary of the Tay, the River Earn. The first available crossing was the Forteviot Bridge, unfortunately just over 6 miles down the road!

So, leaving Perth heading south-west on the B9112 was the best option, which would increase our walk to Glenfarg to 14.5 miles. The first 2 miles through the suburb of Craigie were quite busy with traffic, until we dipped under the motorway, after which it eased off and we could freely march down the road. The countryside was very impressive, quite flat but varied in landscape with wildflowers again in abundance. As we were nearing our long-awaited bridge we came upon what so far had been a rare site...a walker going north. We stopped for a quick chat with him.

"Where are you heading?", I asked.

"John O'Groats ultimately, from Land's End. I've been walking for 8 weeks so far, camping all the way, and have got soaked for most of it. The weather in England has been terrible", he said. I'm not being unkind, but he did look a bit bedraggled.

"Where to next then?" I enquired.

"I'm off to the Cairngorms and will wild camp through them, but I might detour into Aviemore for a break", he said.

We in turn related our walk and recent experiences and then we parted, heading in opposite directions, each of us on our own mission. We took the next left turn and there was the welcome sight of our unremarkable bridge. We had a mile and a half to go before our rendezvous with Rupert at the yet unknown Green of Invermay.

"I'm really looking forward to seeing Rupert again", said Maureen. "I hope he's had a good drive down from the north and won't be delayed".

"Yeh, me too", I said.

The road crossed a railway line and then, just as we reached a farm, we heard a car coming down the road. It was a small white van. As it drew alongside us it slowed right down, and the driver popped his head out of the side window, revealing the unmistakable youthful looks and broad smile of Rupert.

"Hi you two, excellent timing", he said.

"Hiya Rupert", we said in unison, "Great to see you", I continued. "The meeting point is at the junction at the end of this road. We'll be there in about 10 minutes".

"Great, I'll find somewhere suitable to park", he said.

For such a grand title, there is literally one house plus a lodge at the Green of Invermay. The lodge sits in the traditional place at the end of a driveway, this one leading into the Muckersie Estate. What lies beyond the lodge we'll never know, as it's clearly private. But there was a large frontage to the driveway entrance and Rupert had been able to nicely tuck his van against the lodge wall.

He was dressed surprisingly similar to how we'd last seen him in Chamonix in the French Alps. Ever the walking guide, whether on a training course or heading out to Spain, as he was before interrupting his journey south to meet us.

We greeted each other enthusiastically and exchanged heartfelt pleasantries, before Rupert pulled open the rear doors of his van.

"Right", he said, "here's a couple of camping seats for you, as I'm sure you'd welcome getting off your feet for a while. Do you both like Gnocchi? he asked.

"Yes", we chorused, as we kicked off our boots and eased into the seats.

And with that he slid out a two-ringed stove, threw a pan on one ring and proceeded to cook, whilst putting a kettle on the other ring, freshly filled with water from a container stored in the opposite side of the van. Cooking with great confidence, Rupert chatted while he threw in the ingredients, stirring his dish regularly, but simultaneously updating us on his latest guided walk adventures. In what seemed like no time at all he was handing us a dish of piping hot gnocchi, garnished with salad.

Would you like a cup of tea?" Rupert asked.

"We'd prefer coffee, if that's okay", Maureen said, "we're not tea drinkers".

"Oh, well I don't drink coffee, so I never thought to bring any", he said.

Fortunately (top tip coming up!) we have a habit of keeping any surplus coffee sachets from each B&B bedroom and could resolve the apparent dilemma.

It all seemed so very unreal, to be sitting by the roadside outside the lodge of an estate in Scotland eating lunch...we were supposed to be on an arduous walk. I guess it can't be all walk and no play! We could have easily spent the remainder of the day in that position, but after a couple of memorable hours together we had to make our respective moves, ours to Glenfarg and Rupert on his long drive south to catch a ferry. As we were getting our gear together and contemplating the next 7.5 miles to our destination, Rupert had one more act of kindness to offer to us.

"I can drop your rucksacks off at your B&B if you'd like me to. I can go via Glenfarg to pick up the M90", he said.

"That would be fantastic", said Maureen, breathing a noticeable sigh of relief. It was a hot day and anything that made the going easier was very welcome. "We'll fill my rucksack with everything we don't need and just carry Martin's. I'll 'phone the B&B and let them know to expect you".

With his van re-assembled and our boots back on, we were all ready to go our separate ways. There had been no reply at the B&B to Maureen's call, but Rupert said he'd ensure the rucksack was left with someone. And with that we said our goodbyes, not knowing when our paths would cross again. Today had been such a wonderful get together and will always be thought of as a highlight of our walk.

We set off on the quiet lane that would be our route all the way to Glenfarg. Just 10 minutes down the lane and Maureen's mobile rang. It was Rupert.

"I couldn't get an answer when I knocked on the door of the B&B, but the door was open, so I put your rucksack in the lounge behind their settee with a note on the top to say it's yours. It should be safe there", said Rupert.

"That's great, thanks Rupert", Maureen said.

We'd not been too surprised by Rupert's experience at the B&B. It's a refreshing throwback to times long-since gone in England that in the northern parts of Scotland most of the people we'd come across still leave their doors unlocked throughout the day and evening, and only make them secure when they head for their beds. They are very friendly and open people by nature, and so are their doors!

Within a few more miles we found ourselves walking between delightful rolling hills, nothing higher than 350 metres but each one very distinctive. To our right were the Clevage Hills and Ochil Hills, to our left the Dron Hills, and between them were green pastures populated by cows in a variety of colours, interspersed by fields of bright yellow rape seed. Soon the fields became edged with yellow gorse bushes, in this picture book landscape. Between 8 and 14 miles the route was a gradual uphill and we were relieved to summit the final rise before dropping down into the village.

Woodlands B&B was tucked away down a short lane and we duly rang the doorbell. Just as Rupert had discovered there was no reply. We tried the door and it was open, as expected. We shouted our 'hello's', but to no avail. The door to the lounge was open and we could see our rucksack still resident where Rupert had placed it. We returned to the hallway, still shouting, when at last a door opened and we were greeted by our host, Cedric.

"Sorry about that, I was focused on something in my study and I think my wife is on the school run. Welcome to Woodlands. Have you had a good day?", he said.

"Great, thanks", I said. "I see our rucksack is safe and sound".

"What rucksack?", he said. I then told him how Maureen's rucksack came to be in his lounge and, just as we anticipated, he said "oh, we never lock the door, it's always open. Everyone knows everybody around here". We decided against the nightly pub meal as the gnocchi had been very filling. On hearing this Cedric's wife Heather, having returned from the school run, insisted on providing us with a complimentary light snack, which we tucked into once we'd freshened up.

After a good night's sleep, we were up bright and early the following morning as we had a long day ahead of us. Over the past 3 days we'd walked distances of 14, 17 and 14.5 miles, with another 16 miles in store for us today to reach Kirkcaldy.

Yesterday evening we'd exchanged texts with David Kidd from the Country Walking Facebook Group. He lives in the area, near Falkirk, and asked if he could walk with us from Kirkcaldy for the next 2 days. We were delighted that he should want to join us, but we did stress that the day after Kirkcaldy was a sort of 'rest' day, where we walk a shorter distance rather than have a non-walking day. We take this approach for many reasons. Firstly, there's a tendency for lactic acid to build up in joints through inactivity. Secondly, we'd probably end up wandering around wherever we happened to be, so we may as well be walking the route. Finally, a non-walking day would still cost the daily cost of £110, but we wouldn't be making any progress. A few shorter 8-mile days afford a bit of a lie in, a later breakfast, a shorter day of around 4 hours and one where some headway would still be made. David was happy to come along on that basis and we arranged to meet him in our hotel foyer at 9.30am.

We thanked Cedric and Heather for a great stay and marched off down their driveway. The first 2 miles today would again be on a minor lane south, passing through the hamlet of Duncrievie. A local woodworker was selling something called the 'Muckle Chair' and had an example outside, which it had to be for the classically styled four-legged dining chair was an amazing 14 feet high and 6 feet wide! I guess someone will buy it, though Lord knows why. Shortly afterwards we turned left to locate a bridge over the M90. As we crossed we glanced down at the heavy traffic, a brief reminder of the noisy, busy world that we'd escaped from for the 11 weeks we were in our walking bubble.

Maureen was feeling tired today and was walking to a certain extent on autopilot. So far, we'd completed 275 miles over 21 consecutive days of walking, so tomorrow's rest day would be very welcome. Just after 4 miles we turned north briefly to find our next path which would head eastwards into Glen Vale and the Lomond Hills. It was tougher going than expected over the next mile or so, as the winding path ascended the vale towards the John Knox pulpit, something I was keen to see. The pulpit is a cleft in the crags from which John Knox, the Leader of the Reformation in Scotland, used to preach. It was evident where the pulpit had been, but we learned that the rocks themselves were removed in 2004 as they were deemed unsafe. The site is still shown on the OS map and the area is well worth a visit for the landscape alone.

Once over the summit it was a good path down, passing close to the Harperleas Reservoir and 2 miles further on the Holl Reservoir, before walking down the delightfully named Strawberry Avenue to reach the A911 just west of Glenrothes. We carefully walked down this busy road for half a mile before turning left onto our next quiet lane.

About 2/3rds along the lane I noticed a biplane heading across nearby fields over to our right, seemingly in the direction of the coast. "He looks a bit low", I said. It must have turned, for almost immediately the plane skimmed low over our heads as if it had leapt out of some bushes, causing instant profanities to be aired, before it descended into the field to our left and out of sight.

"Keep a look out Maureen, there may be more", I said, anxiously, as we hastened down the lane. A little further on we came to a wide driveway with a sign depicting Fife Airport. A quick glance at the map confirmed its existence. I never knew there was such a thing. You learn something every day on these walks! As we reached the end of this road, having calmed ourselves, I could see ahead that more unexpected excitement was to come.

I'd planned for us to reach Kirkcaldy using what for all intents and purposes should have been a reasonably quiet 'B' road. But I could see a steady stream of traffic coming down that road towards us. By this time, it was 4.30pm and we were both feeling leg weary and generally tired before making this final surge.

"This doesn't look too good", Maureen said, "Isn't there another way?"

"Not really", I said, "Without going quite a way round. It might not be too busy. Perhaps those cars were caught behind a lorry or something", I said, trying my best at appeasement.

Walking single file, I went in front, shouting "car" as the key to us jumping onto the thin grass verge as each vehicle came along. They were very close to us and judging by the occasional horn blasted in our direction, some of the drivers weren't anticipating walkers! About a mile later we came across a farm access road and took refuge there for a few minutes.

"I don't like to suggest this, but it's dangerous and I think we should phone for a taxi", said Maureen. Inwardly I knew she was right from a risk point of view, but from a walk perspective it was a no-no.

"We'll be okay", I assured her. "Let's march on and get the next mile done, by which time there should be a pavement we can use", I said optimistically.

We returned to the grand prix circuit masquerading as a minor public road. Lorries were joining in this game of 'scare the walkers' and doing a very good job of it too! Thrown into the mix now were hidden summits, as the road undulated its way to the highest point. I swear I heard the voice of the immortal Murray Walker, BBC racing commentator, shout more than once into my ear to leap for the verge as "round the bend comes Nigel Mansell in his Ford Mondeo". I must make us more visible, I thought to myself. I decided to hoist my map case as high above my head as possible using an outstretched right arm, which increased my height from a modest 5'7" to an impressive 7'6". It appeared to work, as the last-minute swerves to avoid us seemed to be happening sooner. We safely negotiated the remaining distance until we reached the small hamlet of Cluny, where we found the expected pavement and joined it with a huge sigh of relief.

"That was horrendous", Maureen said, "I'm never doing that again. Next time we do call a taxi".

"Well done babe", I said affectionately and gave her a big hug. It wasn't warmly received, however. Can't say I blamed her, it was a bad experience. If the weather hadn't been so good and it had been raining, it would have been suicidal.

"Let's just get finished now and in the hotel", she said, pointedly.

"Yes, and hopefully there's a package waiting for you there", I said, looking to raise the mood. Maureen's replacement boots that she'd ordered from Cotswolds Outdoors by telephone when we were in Calvine should have arrived if all had gone to plan.

The Dean Park Hotel is situated on the outskirts of Kirkcaldy and before long we were checking in. "You're in room 202 and your parcel is in your room for you, Maureen", said the receptionist in a broad, local accent.

And there they were on the end of a comfortable looking bed. All that remained was to send the faulty pair back to the shop using the same box and packaging that the new ones had arrived in. This would be an on-route task for tomorrow morning.

We awoke to find the rain had returned, though it didn't look to be too heavy. It might even be what the locals call Scotch mist! The new boots had arrived in the nick of time. David Kidd would wing his way to us by train, alighting at Kirkcaldy station some 3 miles across town from us, but he was happy to walk up to meet us and give himself some extra mileage. I looked out of the picture window to see if I could spot him. We'd never met, but I had seen photos of him on the Country Walking Facebook Group pages.

"This must be him now striding across the car park", I said to Maureen. "I hope today is going to be alright, it looks like he walks quite a bit faster than we do", I said.

Walking with friends, new or old, was something we really looked forward to, but it was also a concern. Would they enjoy the day, will the pace be good for them and will they be okay with our comfort breaks and stopping for photos and videos, for example? We decided that with no way of knowing the answers to these concerns up front, we'd have to take the position that people were joining our walk and would need to go with our flow rather than the other way around. Hopefully it would work out okay for everyone.

The bedside phone rang.

"There's a David Kidd in reception for you", said the receptionist.

"Great, many thanks, we'll be down in a few minutes", I said. And with that we picked up our gear and went down to meet him.

David was a tall guy, easily 6 feet plus, and all geared up for the wet weather.

"Hi David, great to meet you", we said in turn. "You're the first person to join us on our walk and it's brilliant of you to give up a couple of days to be with us".

"It's great to be here, despite the weather and I'm looking forward to it", he said. "Call me Dave".

As we donned our waterproofs we explained that a stop off at the local Post Office would be needed and why, but that it was directly on our route. 15 minutes of wet walking later and we were handing the parcel over the Post Office counter before heading for the town centre and sea front. Today's destination was Burntisland, 8 'restful' miles away. It isn't an island, but I'm assured it's pronounced as it reads...Burnt Island. Kirkcaldy, on the other hand, is trickier to pronounce. In fact, I found that however I said it a local, including Dave, would correct me by saying it a different way. I felt sure this was a local tradition, a game probably called 'Toy with the Sassenach visitors', as I never did say it without being corrected! For the record, the town's internet site advises saying it as 'Kirk – Cod – Aaaay'.

Dave explained that he couldn't take a direct train here due to engineering works, but had to take one into Edinburgh and then one out again to Kirkcaldy, resulting in a 40 minutes journey taking 1.5 hours. He would repeat much of this tomorrow to meet us again, so we were grateful that he'd been prepared to take a total of 6 hours by train to be with us for two day's walking.

We decided to take an early coffee break at a town centre cafe, so that we could get to know each other better. Dave told us that he works on an oil rig out in the North Sea, with 3 weeks out there and then 2 weeks shore leave. A tough life and during his working week nowhere to walk! So, he makes the most of every opportunity when he's back on dry land. We think he's brave just taking the helicopter ride to the rig from Aberdeen and back again several times a year.

Kirkcaldy is a tired looking town. It's had an industrial past and used to be known for its production of linoleum. I learnt this from a sketch by Billy Connolly I've got on video at home, in which he also mentions in his colourful way what the smell was like when passengers got off the train at Kirkcaldy during those times. We could tell, even on this damp day, that the linoleum industry no-longer existed! Some well-known politicians are also associated with the town, amongst them former Prime Minister Gordon Brown and David Steel, once joint leader of the Liberal Democrats Party.

After 3 miles we reached the coast, turning west onto the Fife Coastal Path. The rain had all but stopped by now, enabling great views out to sea, where several oil tankers were making their slow progress parallel to the coast. Some oil rigs could also be seen in the distance, though the one Dave works on is a further 80 miles beyond these out to sea. A few parent seals were taking refuge on jagged rocks protruding above the calm waters, whilst their pups were enjoying a swim nearby.

The ensuing 3 miles were due south, initially running behind the beach and then a series of rocks, before reaching the small town of Kinghorn. After rounding the picturesque harbour, we faced a stiff climb up from the sea front via a series of steps. These opened views of the nearby hillside adorned with holiday chalets which overlooked the harbour.

After passing through the edge of town we returned to the coastline and the Firth of Forth, a section of the walk in Scotland that Maureen and I had been particularly being looking forward to, as it culminates with the great spectacle that is the iconic Forth Bridge. That would be another day's walk away yet, to be savoured after a stay in Burntisland, which we reached at 3.30pm. We treated Dave and ourselves to coffees and cakes before he left to catch the train home. Maureen took the opportunity of an early finish to undertake one of her life-essentials, a session at the hair salon! I decided to miss this excitement and look for our B&B which I expected to find just around the corner in the next road. This time it was my turn to have a package waiting for me.

Shouldn't be hard to find, I thought to myself, given that it's known as '39C Cromwell Road'. And it wasn't and soon I was being greeted by Lisa and Dave, the owners.

"Welcome, do come in", said Dave. "Your package is in your room for you", he said. It would contain the next 7 OS maps that would take us through the border with England and as far south as Downham in Lancashire. Our fantastic neighbour in Derby, Brian, was doing a great job of posting the prepared packages on time and so far, they had all been delivered okay. Tomorrow would require another Post Office visit, though Burntisland no-longer has one, so when I booked this B&B Lisa and Dave had kindly offered to take my return package to the next nearest one in Aberdour.

At breakfast, the next morning Lisa asked if she and Dave, plus their Dalmatian dog, could walk the first 4 miles with us to Aberdour. They'd drop the package off at the Post Office and walk home again. We were delighted that they wanted to join us and with Dave Kidd meeting up with us again in town, we'd have a group of five today.

We all gathered outside the cafe we'd visited yesterday and then set off in the bright sunshine for the Fife Coastal Path. Our route took us past the docks and harbour area, where the boats were standing marooned on their underneath fins due to the tide being out. Passing the remains of Rossend Castle, we soon reached a local waterfall cascading down to our path over moss covered rocks and flowing underneath us on its journey to the sea. It was here on day 24 of our journey that we reached 300 miles.

As we continued ahead Maureen and I were talking with 'B&B Dave', when one of those spooky small world instances unfolded. I asked him how he came to be running a B&B in Burntisland. He'd retired back to the area, having be born nearby, but had spent most of his working life in England. "What did you do?" I asked.

"I was a Stress Engineer at Rolls-Royce", he said.

"Which location", I asked, anticipating he'd reply with one of the several company sites in Scotland.

"Derby", he said.

"We worked at Rolls-Royce in Derby", I said. "Which site in Derby were you based at?"

It transpired that not only had Dave worked at the same site as Maureen and me, he also worked in the same building and on the same floor as we did! He'd left there in 1999, but I was there from 1997 and Maureen earlier than that, so without realising it we'd probably passed each other in the Rolls-Royce corridors of power around a couple of decades ago and here we were now, together again! The clear path skirted around the delightful beach at Silversands Bay, before opening out into a park area that had an

73

inviting cafe. We had plenty of time today, so we collectively agreed to have a final coffee together, sitting outside in the glorious weather admiring the views.

We could easily have stayed chatting for hours, but the time came to saddle up again with our rucksacks and head into Aberdour. We parted company with Dave and Lisa outside the Post Office and headed off towards Dalgety Bay. The bay itself comprises mostly of mud flaps, with warning signs advising visitors to keep off, not only because of the dangers of the mud, but because radioactive objects have been found there. The objects come from eroded landfill that contains debris from Second World War aircrafts that originally had radium dials.

As we reached the end of the bay and rounded Hopeward Point, we gained our first sightings of the magnificent Forth Bridge. It was still over 5 miles and 2 hours of walking away yet, but even from that distance it looked impressive. In fact, there has always been two Forth Bridges and a third one is in production for completion in 2017. The classic red bridge, with its three-symmetrical diamond shaped structures spanning the river, is for trains only, with the adjacent Forth Road Bridge used by cars and pedestrians. The new bridge being built would also be for cars.

It was a blue skies day, with the temperature easily 25 degrees and plenty of water was being consumed. We passed through Inverkeithing Bay, evidently an affluent area with huge properties, each with a great view of the bridge and out to sea. The path led up to the edge of Inverkeithing town, before turning due south, still edging along the coast until its end at the North Queensferry Nature Reserve. From there it was a short stretch down the road to our B&B, the Ferrybridge Hotel, which lies just yards away from the towering bridge. Although it was only 3.30pm we insisted on buying Dave a celebratory drink. True to his heritage, Dave is a whisky connoisseur, so we ordered him a double of his chosen tipple.

It had been fantastic walking these last 2 days with Dave, who told us many anecdotes along the way about the places we encountered. As we shook hands and said our goodbyes, he handed Maureen an envelope which we later found contained a very generous donation to our fund-raising efforts. What an all-round great guy – we'd miss him.

After eating in our hotel, we took a stroll in the evening sun for a close view of the bridge. The light was just perfect for showing the bridge off in all its spectacular, red painted glory. Incidentally, the much-used phrase 'it's like painting the Forth Bridge', suggesting something is never-ending, shouldn't be used anymore. Specially developed paint means that rather than the bridge being continuously painted, it now only gets re-painted every 25 years! It towered some 110 metres above us, a steel giant straddling the river since 1890, enabling trains to get in and out of Edinburgh. As we stood there staring at it in awe, we were already looking forward to tomorrow and looking over at it again as we cross the river on its poorer relation.

Here we go. The start at Cape Wrath lighthouse.

Heading for Ullapool.

Meeting Tee Anne in Pitlochry, our first rucksack 'angel'.

Meals on wheels, Rupert cooked lunch for us in his camper van.

Lisa, David and Dave with us on the Fife Coastal path.

The magnificent Forth Bridge.

Chapter 5 – Heading For The Border

We awoke to an overcast day. It's amazing the difference light and sunshine makes to a view, the different contrasts and perspectives that it gives. An overcast day however, tends to flatten the view and make it almost monotone. We were thankful therefore, to have marvelled at the Forth Bridge in yesterday's evening sunlight. Today the bridge looked as magnificent as it will always do, one of those structures that you can easily stare at all day long, though the brightness of its red coat was now more subdued under a veil of dark clouds.

A short stroll through North Queensferry led to a flight of steps that took us up onto the Forth Road Bridge. The third bridge, to be known as the Queensferry Crossing, remained under construction when we passed through, a standard modern looking structure. Our excitement grew as we began to walk across, the magnificent Forth Bridge to our left dwarfing the village below, with one of the day's 120 trains just travelling across it. An ocean cruise liner was slowly drifting by the bridge, no doubt to afford its passengers the opportunity to see this awesome piece of engineering excellence before setting out to sea again. As we continued our crossing we came to a double section of the safety fencing that was festooned with colourful padlocks, a practice begun by two romantics in Paris in 2008, who declared their love for each other by attaching a padlock on the Pont des Arts bridge over the River Seine. Millions of others have copied this on various bridges around the world, including us!

We almost didn't want this moment to end by reaching the other side, but a 10 mile walk to the unusually named Currie on the outskirts of Edinburgh was our goal for the day. Alas, South Queensferry soon approached and we dropped down a flight of stairs from the bridge into the village area. After a few checks against our map, plus asking for directions from a local guy in this small but confusing district, we finally managed to find cycle route 76. As with most cycle routes it was a disused rail track, which unfortunately can sometimes be long, straight and boring, but they do keep you away from busy roads.

An hour or so further on and our good friend the sun reappeared and would be with us for the remainder of the day. At 4 miles, we came to what I tend to call an 'intersection with modern life' and all the noise that is usually associated with it. We were on the outskirts of Scotland's capital city after all. The M9 motorway sidled across from the right to meet us, while over to our left were uninterrupted views across open fields to the runways of Edinburgh Airport. Although this was a Sunday, the planes were queuing for take-off in their disciplined and orderly manner. Our path passed within a few metres of the perimeter fence at the south end of the runway, before reaching the A8 at Ratho Station. As we turned to walk a few hundred yards along this busy bypass to a footbridge, with the planes roaring in and out of the airport to our left, this could easily have been the height of a normal working day rather than the Sabbath. However, a couple of miles further on and we had left it all behind, now walking on a canal towpath in rural calmness. It was very warm by now, so we took a break and kicked off our boots for a while.

We left the canal at Gogar Moor Bridge after 7.5 miles, with quiet back lanes used for the remainder of the walk into the district of Currie, located a couple of miles south-east of Edinburgh. We were aiming for the Riccarton Arms for our overnight stay. We'd stayed there before in 2012, coincidentally on the day that Edinburgh's two major football teams, Hibernian (Hibs) and Heart of Midlothian (Hearts), were meeting in a Scottish Cup Final for the first time since 1896. The pub was crammed with Hearts supporters watching the match on a big screen and much to our relief, their team comprehensively won the match and therefore the cup. I hate to think what kind of a night we might have had if they'd have lost! No such issues this time around though and a pleasant, uneventful stay was enjoyed.

A misty start was encountered the following morning, with the distant Pentland Hills barely visible. Hopefully the gloom would lift as I was particularly looking forward to walking over these hills. We'd previously walked through them on a walk at ground level, but not over them. So, whilst the route to Carlops was 11.5 miles, it would be a tough day worth more like 15 miles in terms of effort on our legs.

An initial steep climb out of Currie took us onto the moors. The mist was clearing slowly, but was still sufficiently evident to give the moors a classic damp and mysterious appearance. The path descended after a mile or so down to Glencrose Reservoir. It was quiet next to the reservoir, with tethered boats projecting a mirror image onto the still water and the whole place had an air of peaceful tranquillity to it. At the far end of the reservoir we turned right to head up onto the Pentland Hills. It was a very steep, arduous introduction to these hills and we were soon both finding it hard going. Maureen was having some difficulties carrying her rucksack, so I took it over for a while. "It'll be okay once we're up", I reassured her.

In planning this route, I knew there were 5 summits to the Pentland Hills. The views from the top would be glorious, in good weather. My research had indicated that once we were up the first hill the path would undulate across them. It would be straightforward walking for 5 miles before taking a steep descent back to ground level. Unfortunately, the reality was quite different. Between each summit the path dropped several hundred metres and then rose again, making for 5 significant ascents. I should hold my hand up and admit I'd got it completely wrong!

Maureen was understandably not a happy bunny. Indeed, you'd probably struggle to find a bunny in the mood she was now in that could express itself as vociferously and with such a volume of expletives as Maureen let fly in my direction. I knew that in part it was induced by back pain and tiredness, but nevertheless it was warranted if I'm honest. In going to these hills, it was nothing like the Sound of Music! We argued for what seemed endless miles and had spells walking several metres apart. But on the plus side good progress was being made. Usually when we argue our walking speed increases significantly!

"This next hill, Scald Law, is the highest summit. After that it should be downhill", I said, trying in vain to win a Nobel Peace Prize. As we reached and looked over the top, shock horror, it wasn't. There were two more elements of this roller coaster to go, taking in East Kip and West Kip. Even I, 'Mr Pragmatic' (well, let's just get it done) wasn't enjoying the day now and longed to see a clear path to Carlops and the sanctuary of our B&B. The mist had thankfully burnt off during all this excitement and there were great views back to Edinburgh, though I was the only one taking much notice by now.

At 9 miles, the path did finally descend off the hills and a generally speechless final 2 miles or so on a back lane led us to our B&B, the Allan Ramsey Hotel. "Please God, let it be a great stay", I said to myself as we went to the bar to check-in...it wasn't!

We'd stayed at this hotel in 2012 and as far as we remembered it was okay. It's the only place around, so we had no choice but to eat in. It was good pub grub, but at A La Carte prices it was not the best value for money. Sometimes it's a case of having to pay the going rate. Whilst the atmosphere had calmed from the earlier ructions, the higher-than-average meal costs didn't help matters. Worse was to come, however!

We woke the next morning to a bright, sunny day. A quick shower then breakfast was needed before setting out on a long 16.5 miles to Peebles. I switched the shower on, but nothing happened. I tried the sink taps and again nothing. I made a call downstairs on the room telephone to find out that there was no running water anywhere in the village due to a pipe burst. There was a cold tap in the toilets near the bar that was giving a very small amount of water out, so we each had a quick, cold wash before eating. The hotel owners, whilst not to blame for the burst pipe, were not going out of their way to improve the situation by repeatedly saying there was nothing they could do. After breakfast, we settled our inflated bill and asked if, given that we couldn't fill our water bottles from a tap, we could possibly take three bottles of water from the bar fridge. "I'll have to charge you £2 per bottle", said the owner. I thought they might offer them to us without charge as a goodwill gesture, but they didn't, so we declined them. Maureen saw red and it was all I could do to get her out of the door and on the road, but I did.

We set off in glorious sunshine down a quiet lane for the first 4 miles, with much gentler scenery surrounding us, consisting of open fields, numerous sheep farms and plenty of forestation. At the busy A701 we turned left, with no option but to walk against the busy traffic and hop onto the narrow grass verge whenever possible. We'd only be on this for 1.5 miles, but it wouldn't be pleasant. After half a mile, I noticed an access lane running parallel to us and with a bit of a struggle through gorse and a low hedge, we could get on it and away from the traffic, albeit for a short distance. A little way along this lane we shouted 'hello' to a smart looking couple doing a spot of gardening.

"Are you going far", asked John, who was unusually well dressed for gardening, sporting a jacket and tie.

"Peebles today", I replied.

"Fancy a coffee? Come and take a seat in the garden and we'll make you one". It took us a bit by surprise, but we decided to take them up on their kind gesture. "Four coffees please, Margaret", he said to his wife. Maureen asked if she could use their toilet and followed Margaret into their house. Some 15 minutes later they both returned, Margaret carrying a tray of coffees and cakes.

"I've just been given a tour of the house, it's marvellous inside", said Maureen.

It all seemed a bit unreal, the four of us sitting on chairs on their front lawn, chatting away, eating cake and drinking coffee; we were supposed to be on a long-distance walk! After recent events, it felt good to be pampered.

"Now, you can't walk up the A701, it's far too dangerous", said John. "I'll give you a lift to the next lane", he insisted. I don't like to miss any of the intended walking route, but as it was only a mile and it made sense from a safety point of view, I reluctantly accepted. I'm sure we'd more than make up the 'lost' mile at some point before reaching Dover. "Do you want to take some water with you?" John asked.

That would be great, we're a little low on it", I said. Within no time John emerged from his garage with a pack of 12 bottles.

"Here you go", he said, "take them all".

"That's amazingly generous of you, but we can't carry that amount", Maureen replied. "But we will take four if that's okay". She then told him of our hotel bottled water saga.

The water safely stored in the side pockets of our rucksacks we turned to head for the car. Now the thing was, John had a beautiful looking Jaguar parked on the driveway. We were two hot, not particularly aromatic walkers who hadn't had a shower that morning, getting into a spotless Jaguar. Rucksacks in the boot, we thanked Margaret for her hospitality and we were off. In a matter of minutes, we were getting out again, safely delivered to the next back lane and saying our goodbyes to John.

"What a brilliant couple", I said to Maureen. "Absolutely", she said. "Margaret invited us to come back sometime and spend a week with them". How amazing, given that we were 2 strangers just passing by who they'd never met before. It was very refreshing to meet such kind people, we thought.

The walk continued in much the same vein as earlier, a nice quiet lane with little in the way of traffic and pleasant, if unspectacular, scenery. At such times Maureen is prone to putting headphones on and listening to Steve Wright on Radio 2 (whatever turns you on!). When someone wearing headphones speaks they tend to be very loud to hear themselves talking. As we were passing through a quiet hamlet Maureen announced to the local inhabitants, "I need to stop somewhere for a wee". Fortunately, there were few people at home to hear her proclamation.

We turned onto a footpath for the final 2 miles, a former drove road skirting round our only climb of the day, the modest Hamilton Hill. It wasn't particularly steep or high, but it did provide a great vantage point for looking down onto Peebles nestled in the valley below. The path gradually descended through a mass of bright yellow gorse bushes to reach town. We were now well and truly in the Scottish Borders, with Peebles being the largest town in the area. Its name means "a place where tents are pitched". I'm sure they are, especially on the banks of the River Tweed, but we'd got a cosy night booked in Rowanbrae B&B.

Breakfast TV the following morning confirmed it was Wednesday 1st June. My original aim was to have crossed the border into England by now, but refinements to the route when I was pre-booking our accommodation meant an extra 4 days in

Scotland. The month of May had been brilliant weather-wise, with only 1.5 days of rain and temperatures in the high twenties most of the time. The heat had meant drinking significant amounts of water each day. Despite this Maureen started today not feeling too well as a bout of cystitis was flaring up. She was in two minds whether to walk at all, but her inner strength and determination won the day. We decided to aim for Traquair, 7 miles away, where we'd stop to see how she was. It was the only real stopping place on today's long 18.5 mile walk to a tiny place called Hartleap. Maureen needed to feel confident she'd make it from there.

The weather was dry and warm, although cloudy, as we set off to cross the bridge over the River Tweed. The B7062 was our method for reaching Traquair, a seldom used road by traffic and one that is perched above the river most of the way affording great views across the valley to the hills beyond. A huge hotel and golfing complex sits on the opposite bank of the river at Cardrona – there's no shortage of golf courses in Scotland! The sun was out by now and the temperature rising again as we glanced over towards the nearby town of Innerleithen. Our water supplies were diminishing quickly, especially as Maureen needed to keep drinking to help clear the cystitis. We came upon a lodge at the gates to Traquair House, a 12th-century stately home set on a 4,000-acre estate. It is also Scotland's Oldest Inhabited House, which has been lived in for over 900 years. The occupier happened to come out as we were passing, so we cheekily asked if she would fill up our two already empty water bottles, which she was happy to do.

Traquair village was soon reached, so we took an early lunch there, taking advantage of a handy bench. Maureen felt 'okay' to continue, so with rucksacks back on we changed road to the B709, which would take us all the way to Hartleap. The route became a gradual climb to 11.5 miles, the road surrounded by plantations for most of the way, with only occasional glimpses of the wider countryside possible. Hamlets and properties were fewer and further apart and as we walked we had that feeling of being progressively more isolated.

The previous evening in Peebles I'd telephoned our B&B host at Hartleap, Lindsay, who confirmed she would be back from an appointment in Selkirk by the time we arrived and that she may well pass us by on her journey home. Sure enough, at 12 miles a car pulled alongside us and the lady driver said, "Are you Martin and Maureen by any chance?"

"Yes, hi Lindsay, good to see you", I said.

"Would you like me to take your rucksacks?", she offered.

"That would be great", Maureen replied, and on this occasion both rucksacks went. The last 5 miles felt so different after 30 days of carrying them! As Lindsay drove away we headed downhill to the crossroads by the derelict Gordon Arms, followed by a level walk along the valley bottom.

We reached Hartleap around 5pm. Lindsay's large dormer bungalow sits away from the road behind a long front garden and is surrounded by land on all sides. No neighbours, it was a real get-away-from-it-all place. We would be eating in that night. I would describe Lindsay as in the mould of Germaine Greer, with greying hair, round glasses and being a very assured, knowledgeable person. The accommodation was comfortable but quirky in two ways. As we went up the stairs to be shown to our room there was various artwork on the walls. One of these was of an obese, headless, naked lady, leaving nothing to the imagination other than what the lady may have looked like. It seemed a strange painting to have on the stairs where guests pass through, we thought. But the strangest thing was to come. The bedroom was en-suite, but dividing the main room from the toilet and shower area was a thin, white, transparent lace curtain. Now call us old fashioned, but when either of us uses the loo we'd rather not be seen or heard! Hence when we did use it one of us would have to leave the room and wait on the landing outside until the 'all clear' was given. I'd also not picked up that this was a vegetarian establishment, but the fish dinner was nonetheless very enjoyable. The quirks apart, it was a very comfortable stay in an idyllic setting. Lucky Lindsay.

The next morning, we awoke in the knowledge that it would be the longest walking day of our entire route. Thankfully Maureen was feeling good and it seemed that her waterworks issues had abated.

We were soon back on the B709. It might seem that much of Scotland was spent walking on roads, and indeed it was. Some 2/3rds of the 410 miles through Scotland, roughly 273 miles, were covered on roads, plus many more miles on tarmac cycle paths. This was out of the ordinary for us as, like most walkers, we spend our time trekking on footpaths over the countryside. But this was no ordinary walk and north-south footpaths just don't come along in Scotland too often. There was no doubt that the hard ground, while necessary, was beginning to take its toll on our legs.

The first 6.5 miles to Ettrick were a mirror of the end to yesterday's walk in terms of the terrain. From Ettrick onwards, the road downgraded to a single track with passing places for cars, not that many came along in this progressively more remote area. In fact, the only traffic encountered was the occasional logging lorry which roared past with the latest batch of logs to have been felled. Other than these, the tranquillity was only disturbed by the occasional birdsong. We were now surrounded by beautiful rolling hills and emerald green fields of grass, separated by a snaking ice blue river that trailed us along the valley. There wasn't a cloud in the sky and the heat was progressively rising through the day. It was a very flat terrain, great to walk in and to get the miles under our belts. Maureen did though, resort to another session of 'Steve Wright in the afternoon' on Radio 2. Thankfully, she didn't burst into song at any point!

Despite its name the Scottish Borders don't reach the border with England, but lead into Dumfries and Galloway which holds that honour. A signpost at 12 miles confirmed our arrival there, with the road now heading downhill into Eskdalemuir. 4 miles further on we turned a corner and came to a sight we'd both been really looking forward to. We sort of knew what to expect, but the sheer nature of it being so out of context with all that we'd seen in Scotland still took us by surprise.

There before us was the Kagyu Samye Ling Tibetan Buddhist Centre, the first to have been established in the West in 1967 and still to this day the biggest one outside of Tibet! Huge golden Buddhist figures adorn the grounds close to the road. A white tower was topped with golden symbols from which long strands of bunting stretched to the ground in five different directions. We ventured down the driveway, lined with white lanterns, to take a brief look around. Several of the 60 monks that permanently reside there passed us by, seemingly on their way to the main temple, whilst a group of visitors were heading towards some nearby trees, each with a curved wooden sword, presumably to experience a Buddhist ritual. It's a huge estate and unfortunately, we only had the briefest of glimpses into what it offers, but we resolved to return for a full visit one day.

Just 3 miles remained now to reach our accommodation at Watcarrick, a working farm set back from the road and fortunately, one that offered evening meals due to its remote location. In fact, on arrival after being warmly greeted by Jock and Sara, we were asked what we would like for dinner, a bit like your parents might do! We opted for the chicken curry and then went off to our room to freshen up.

Later, after a lovely meal, I put my usual telephone call through to our next B&B, partly to ensure they were expecting us but also to check out an aspect of our route. My aim was to turn off the B709 at Paddockhole Bridge and use a couple of farm tracks across a hillside to reach the minor lane just north of Torbeckhill, where their B&B was located.

"I'd best double-check that's okay for you with the farmer, as I know there's been some issues with walkers around that area", said Gordon, our next host. In a matter of minutes, he was back to me. "No can do", he said, "The farmer says 'no' due to security issues with some walkers posting pictures of his farm on the internet", Gordon said. "Best if you stay on the road and if you've had enough walking I can drive to pick you up, as it's a longer way round by the road".

"That's very kind of you Gordon, but we should be okay", I replied. "See you tomorrow".

The sun was up early the following morning. We decided that after three long days of walking we'd ease into the day. It was 12.5 miles to Torbeckhill on flat roads, so it shouldn't take too long to complete. As we reached the bottom of the farm's long driveway another walker was just coming along, though not a traditional looking backpacker. He was casually dressed in shorts, lightweight jacket and open sandals, with a large brimmed hat and was using a staff rather than a walking stick. He looked for all intents and purposes like a pilgrim. We spoke for a few minutes and he told us that he had just left the Buddhist Centre after 2 years there, one year of which he never left his room while he 'found' himself.

"Well, it's a glorious day to be out and about. Have a good walk", I said, inferring that we wouldn't wish to delay him any longer! In any case we needed to spend a few minutes re-tying our boots, we convinced ourselves. He seemed harmless enough, but we decided it would be best to let him get a distance ahead of us, all the same.

Maureen wasn't feeling 100% unfortunately. Her cystitis had flared up in the night and she was still feeling the effects of it. To add insult to injury, as we set off in earnest her left knee became 'clicky'. It improved after a couple of miles, but the cystitis wasn't going to go away in a hurry and was becoming increasingly more painful.

The scenery around us, in what was now the Esk Valley, was similar to previous days, a gentle mixture of grassy fields, plantation trees and the winding River Esk, a delightful blue, reflecting the clear sky above us. The temperature was rising quickly and by noon it was a scorcher, with virtually no shade anywhere to gain any respite. We had 6 bottles of water with us and we would need them all before reaching our destination.

We took breaks every 3 miles. With the sun beating down on us, Maureen was feeling progressively worse. "I don't think I'm going to make it", she said at our 9 miles stop. We were effectively in the middle of nowhere, no houses or farms to try to get help, no passing cars to flag down and Maureen's energy draining fast. She soldiered on for 2 more miles, but by then was not far off fainting. We came to a few trees that provided a little shade and an opportunity to rest and it was there that fortune shined on us. Maureen's mobile bleeped indicating that, to our amazement, it had a signal. Despite what network operators suggest, our experiences after walking in many areas of the UK are that once outside of town areas signals are a rarity. But not now, so I called Gordon at the B&B. I explained how unwell

Maureen was and where we were. "I'll come straightaway and collect you. Give me 10 minutes", he said.

"I'm really sorry, but I'm in severe pain", said Maureen.

"Don't be sorry or worry", I said, "Health always comes first. The priority is to get you out of this heat and address your cystitis". Knowing how Maureen hates to not finish what we set out to do I said, "We've virtually done 12 miles so we're not far short of the day's target and we'll no doubt make up the remainder by going wrong at some point, I'm sure".

Gordon's car soon pulled up in front of us. He leapt out and took our rucksacks, dropping them into the car boot and then we were off. "It's not far, soon be there", he said as we recounted to him the day's experiences. He came to halt outside a large, secluded bungalow where his wife Yvonne was waiting on the doorstep. "Hi, I've got you in to see my doctor in Annan in 30 minutes time", she said to Maureen. "Gordon will take you straight there and bring you back afterwards", she said.

"Brilliant, many thanks", we said. The three of us were soon shooting down the road for the 8-mile drive to Annan. No sooner had we sat down in the waiting area than Maureen was called through to see the doctor. Shortly she was back with me with a prescription for antibiotics in her hand and a flea in her ear from the doctor, who said that she was significantly dehydrated and must drink at least 3 litres of water per day. We collected the pills from the nearby chemist, after which Gordon duly drove us back to the B&B.

Gordon and Yvonne had been amazing. We had been so lucky to have been heading for them when all of this happened. The stay at their B&B also turned out to be the best of the entire walk. The bungalow was a former farm house, with views out over the farm fields that still surrounded it, with the Solway Firth and the northern hills of the Lake District in the distance. The evening meal was amazing, and our room had every facility you could wish for, including luxurious dressing gowns (always a big bonus in Maureen's eyes). If ever you're looking for accommodation just over of the border into Scotland, look no further than Torbeckhill B&B.

Mercifully the next morning Maureen was feeling much better and felt able to walk our final day in Scotland. After a great breakfast Gordon drove us down their long drive to the minor road that we'd be using for most of the 11.5 miles to Gretna. The weather was warm and dry, but overcast, with no signs of a scorcher in the forecast, so hopefully a straightforward day's walking lay ahead of us.

We were now in Annandale, which if anything was even more sedate an area than the Esk Valley. This was no bad thing, as in a couple of days we'd be in the Lake District, where the terrain would be off-road and significantly different. The miles were soon ticked off and before long we were looking ahead to being in Gretna Green, a separate village to its larger neighbour Gretna and of course noted for its history of runaway teenage weddings. The famous Blacksmiths Shop is where couples have gone to marry since 1754, taking advantage of Scotland's lenient marriage laws.

We reached Gretna Green at 2pm and, as if it had been scripted especially for us, a wedding had just taken place. The bride and groom, plus their guests, were all gathered in the area outside the Blacksmiths Shop, most of the men wearing kilts representing different clans, and of course there was the obligatory piper. We stopped for coffee to watch proceedings, which included the newlyweds posing for photographs underneath a wooden arch shaped in the form of two arms stretching skywards, where the hands joined some 15 feet above, representing lovers together.

We stayed there a full hour and had a good look around the various historical buildings and shops, before heading down the road for the final 20 minutes stint to our B&B. Once there we sat outside in the warm sun, with a further couple of coffees, reflecting on the fact that we'd completed our journey through Scotland.

It had been a wonderful 31 days of walking, covering 410 miles, in fantastic weather in the main, with only 1.5 days of rain...unbelievable. We'd started at Cape Wrath on 5th May, walked through the Highlands, the Cairngorms, Perth and Kinross, through the Borders and then Dumfries and Galloway to the foot of Scotland. We were almost at the border with England. So far, so good, we thought.

Chapter 6 – From Lochs To Lakes

Sunday 5th June dawned with bright sunshine, and ahead of us probably the shortest walk we'd ever do or were ever likely to do again in Scotland.

Just 300 yards from our B&B was the border with England. We couldn't physically see it as we set off, but a short stretch down the first road and a right turn would bring it into view. What great landmark awaited us, we wondered, how was this significant point on the UK map distinguished from anywhere else? The B7076 has the honour of transporting into England all who travel along it in a southerly direction. The first indication of the border came in the form of The Old Toll Bar Cafe, whose two-sided angled sign states it is the 'last house in Scotland' for those, like us, heading south, or from the other side that it is the 'first house in Scotland'. Built in 1830, it proclaims that over 10,000 weddings have been held there.

Although Maureen really enjoyed Scotland, being back in England gave her a psychological boost. Being away from family and friends for the last 5 weeks had been difficult for her. Now she could look forward to seeing some of them in a couple of weeks' time as we venture ever further south.

The road climbed a little, we passed over the River Sark and there it was, a standard size sign mounted on the grass verge saying no more than 'Welcome to England & Cumbria', incorporating graphics of the English flag and the motif for Cumbria County Council. I expected something grander that this, perhaps something historic looking like a castle gateway and mock portcullis or an archway over the road perhaps, not a rather bland road sign. Perhaps this had to be a politically correct sign, identical to the one across the road for those venturing north?

The thunderous M6 was now a near neighbour, with our minor road, thankfully, a significantly poorer relation in terms of traffic. The noise was a short-lived intrusion until the 2 miles point where, after crossing the River Esk, we took a sharp right turn inland on the Cumbria Coastal Way. Lovely though this sounds, it is unfortunately a seldom used footpath that was equally seldom maintained, being overgrown and instantly hard work to make progress on. An early exit was called for, so a swift look at the OS map revealed the option to nip down a short lane and join cycle route 7 once more.

We enjoyed the solitude of our quiet lane until just over 5 miles when we reached the village of Rockcliffe. This provided an instant dose of patriotism with the very first gardens displaying mannequins of members of the royal family, supporting the village's forthcoming celebrations of the Queen's official birthday on 11th June (her actual birthday being 21st April). Apparently, the monarch traditionally has two birthdays so that the celebratory military parade known as 'Trooping the Colour' on Horse Guards Parade in London can take place in (hopefully) good weather.

After taking a snack break in the local churchyard, always a good place for finding a bench, we continued in the now very hot sun to reach Carlisle. The suburbs were a pleasant surprise, featuring impressive Victorian style housing, which led us to re-joining the Cumbria Coastal Path for a short while at the River Eden.

The path eased away from the river and took us by the local cricket ground, which was set in an amphitheatre below us, where a match was in progress. Spectators were sitting in their fold-up chairs around the boundary consuming ice creams and cold drinks, and it was all rather, well, English!

We crossed a bridge over the river to mix with the inevitable city traffic as we travelled along the hot pavement in search of our

B&B. We arrived just after 3pm to find the owner seemingly not in the best of moods.

"Oh, you're here", he said, "I was expecting you earlier".

"I don't know that we'd said a time particularly", I replied. "I don't remember being asked to give one. Is there a problem?" I asked.

"Nor, nor, come in", he said in his strong northern accent. He proceeded to give us our room key while telling us he needed to go out for a while. We just wanted to get this bit over with and get freshened up after our hot walk. He finished by saying what I heard as, "if you need Wi-Fi there's a cord on the fridge".

He instantly left for whatever pressing engagement we'd evidently made him late for. "What was that last bit?" Maureen asked.

I repeated "if you need Wi-Fi there's a cord on the fridge. I'll try to figure it out once I've got this rucksack off and shed some of this gear", I suggested as we entered our room. My latest parcel of maps had arrived okay and was on the bed next to the traditional pyramid of towels. After taking a shower, I decided to have a roam around the establishment, still uttering to myself "if you need Wi-Fi there's a cord on the fridge". Nothing on the ground floor provided an answer, so I went up to the next level above ours and there on the landing, unusually, stood a fridge in a small alcove. I looked inside and there was some fresh milk and chilled water. As I closed the door I noticed on the top a hand-written note on a piece of paper that said, "Wi-Fi code". The penny dropped. When I heard him say 'cord' in his strong accent he was saying "code". I think though, even Sherlock would have failed to decipher that he also meant there was a fridge on the first-floor landing with a piece of paper on it, on which the Wi-Fi code was written!

I returned to our room, triumphant in my detective work, to reveal the solution to the mystery statement to Maureen. Duty bound to now use the Wi-Fi, we posted updates of our walk onto the Country Walking Facebook Group, answered and sent a few texts, then went out for dinner.

Next morning, we went down to breakfast wondering what the atmosphere might be like. Mr Grumpy had already left for his day job and his wife Lynn was doing the breakfast honours. If she had also been in a bad mood yesterday she had clearly gotten out of the bed on the right side and gave us a cheerful greeting. "Help yourself to cereals and I'll be back with your coffee in a jiffy", she said. Having filled our bowls, we looked for the milk, but couldn't readily spot any near the cereals. Maureen looked to see if any of the other tables had milk. The adjacent one did, so she helped herself and dutifully returned what seemed an unusual bottle to its place of origin. Almost instantly the allocated guests for that table arrived, as did Lynn with our coffees.

"Oh, you haven't any milk have you", she said, and went over to (yet another) fridge, this one secreted out of sight in the corner of the room, to retrieve some for us.

Almost in the same movement she swivelled to greet the other guests and said to one lady "I've put your special milk out on the table for you, as you can see". I looked across at Maureen in horror, who equally looked across at me with the same question clearly in both our minds – what was special about the milk that Maureen had just poured over her Weetabix? Would she be ill halfway to Caldbeck? With respect to the lady concerned, we could discount breast milk, but what else could it be? With perfect timing, the consumer from the opposite table said, "I can only drink soya milk, so I have to bring my own with me". Thank God for that, we both thought.

Although we'd got a 14 mile walk to Caldbeck today, we again decided to take advantage of being in a large town to visit a few shops. I dropped into the Post Office with my return package of maps for sending home, whilst Maureen picked up some lunch for us. It was a typical town centre, plenty of paved areas and the usual array of familiar shops, but nevertheless I found it again a pleasant surprise. Next task was to find the Market Cross, a column shaped monument on a square base set upon 5 circular steps. It marks the start of the Cumbria Way, a long distance 70-mile route running north to south mostly through the Lake District, ending at Ulverston on Morecambe Bay. We would be walking for 3 days on this before necessarily turning eastwards.

The initial route through the town took us past its medieval cathedral and on towards the 900-year-old Carlisle Castle, before taking the more modern Millennium Footbridge over the River Caldew. Once over, the path turned left to weave through a small industrial area before embarking on open countryside. It was a lovely sunny day to begin with and became progressively hotter as the miles were ticked off. By noon the temperature had risen to 27 degrees, which we later learned had made Carlisle and its surrounding area the hottest place in the UK that day. We'd stocked up on sun protection cream in Carlisle and were already making regular use of it.

Despite the challenge of the heat, all was going well, on very flat terrain, as our route followed the course of the River Caldew, which it would do all the way to Caldbeck. We crossed over a lane at Rose Bridge and in the subsequent mile endured consecutive 'cow moments'. We'd walked 410 miles through Scotland with only one such experience and here we were, 20 miles into England, and we had to face two separate herds of Holsteins. Both were directly on our footpath, with no real way around them other than to backtrack to Rose Bridge to take a lane diversion that would add 4 – 5 miles to our day.

Sometimes when faced with this situation it's a case of having a bit of patience, as it was with the first herd. They slowly moved across our intended path, giving us their steely eye as they did, until heading away, but we had to wait 10 – 15 minutes for them to fully pass. It was, though, an opportunity to take our rucksacks off. Once the last cow was safely out of our way we crossed the stile and carried on, with an occasional backwards glance to ensure they'd lost any interest they might have had in us.

We'd no sooner gathered our composure again when, after following a bend in the riverside path, we saw the next Holsteins waiting for us on the other side of the next stile. There was no going back from this point, other than as a very last resort, so we took our tried and tested approach of weighing up the situation from this relatively safe distance before deciding what to do. Whilst there were plenty of them, they seemed sedate enough. There were no youngsters among the group, nor any energetic teenagers who might be inclined to chase us, but these more mature cows were just where we didn't want them to be, across the path to our escape stile 200 yards away.

"What do you think?" Maureen asked.

"I think we give the first batch a wide berth, then cut back across to the fence where the stile is. Those sitting close to the stile seem happy to be chewing the cud, so I think we should do it", I said. We crossed the stile and entered their domain. Their chilling stares were made in our direction but, just as with the fabled gorgon, you're okay if you don't stare back. We walked briskly, but not so fast as to appear to be running at them, and made it past the first cows. Our heartbeats were racing as we followed the plan and steered a course towards the stile. The seated cows all but ignored us as we sidled through them and reached sanctuary. I stood guard, walking stick at the ready, while Maureen made her safe escape, then I made mine. On this

100

occasion, as on many to come, the thought of what might happen is what creates the anxiety. With a good assessment of the risks before entering a field and taking a wide berth where possible, passing cows will usually go without a hitch...but you must be careful!

At 10 miles, our path reached a lane where we should have crossed the river using the Bell Bridge to continue to the opposite bank. Recent torrential rain and severe flooding, ironically as we were enjoying hot and cloudless days in Scotland, had caused the bridge to collapse into the river. We could resort to a lane alternative for the next mile and then pick up our footpath again.

By 3pm the sun had decided to call it a day and the sky started to cloud over. It remained very humid, with the temperature not really abating. For the next 2 miles, the path meandered through Dentonside Wood, with the river having reduced in size to become the Cald Beck, from which our destination takes its name. As we approached the village we could see rain clouds gathering and then heard a few rumbles of thunder. Almost instantly the first flashes of lightening streaked across the sky.

"Let's hope we get finished before the inevitable rain comes", I said to Maureen. My hope was in vain. The first heavy spots of rain soon arrived and became faster and faster. We donned our waterproofs just in time, as Him upstairs turned on the power shower and threw in gale force winds as a bonus. It was unbelievable how the weather changed in a matter of minutes. With difficulty seeing our way forward we plodded on into the village, buffeted by the wind. I expected our B&B, The Old Rectory, to be just around the first bend, but it wasn't. The scene in the village was like something you might see on the TV news, where a storm is lashing torrential rain onto those unfortunate to find themselves in it, pushing them in every direction but the one they wish to go in.

We'd seemingly come into the village on a different path to the one I'd planned, and we now needed to know where to go next. In desperation, we dived into the narrow doorway of a house, which barely took us out of the elements, wiped the rain from the map case and checked where we were.

"Just round to the right and we're there", I shouted to Maureen above the incessant noise of wind and rain. We stepped out, heads down, and charged off down the road, where 150 yards later the driveway to the B&B was found. It was a lovely, though disappointingly long driveway in these conditions, but we made it to the porch. The front door was open and we were instantly greeted by our host, Anne, who had been looking out for us. Her husband Tim joined her from one of the many rooms to the rear of the hallway.

"Come straight in, don't worry about the rain", she said. "Drop your waterproofs in this basket and we'll sort them out for you", she beckoned. We were so happy to get out of them and the rain.

This was an accommodation I'd been looking forward to. The Old Rectory, as is often the case with church houses, was huge. It was a two-storey manor house with five windows across the front and a central feature doorway through which we'd just entered. A large hall led to a sweeping staircase, up which we were dutifully led by Tim to our room. The bedroom was full of character and a floor that creaked as I walked across. It was so uneven that I struggled to walk in a straight line at first. A large mirror hung from a picture rail over the ornate fireplace. The wardrobes looked antique and creaked as we opened them. I went over to the picture window and peered out over the English country garden below. As I looked out I could see that the rain had already stopped. The storm had been short-lived, but would never be forgotten in the annals of our walking experiences!

As we freshened up we discussed tomorrow's walk, a 14-mile stint to Keswick, which included 'bagging a Wainwright' on the way. It would be a tough one and Maureen didn't like the thought of carrying her rucksack if it was going to be another very hot day. One of the advantages of being on a recognised trail like the Cumbria Way is that they tend to get supported by baggage moving companies. So, I went online to check this out and contacted a firm called Brigantes, who could take a rucksack to Keswick for £20. "I think it's worth the cost if it helps protect your back for a day and gets us to Keswick", I said. Maureen readily agreed, and we made the booking. When I put in my usual advance call to our next B&B I checked that someone would be there to take delivery at the expected time of its arrival.

Despite having enjoyed a classic pub meal of pie and chips in The Oddfellows Arms, the next morning we were still looking forward to a hearty breakfast in Anne's traditional country kitchen, a room with a high ceiling from which hung a Victorian kitchen maid dryer above the stylish range. Whilst we ate cereals at the large wooden table, Anne cracked open the eggs from their own chickens and chatted with us as she cooked them. Interestingly, we couldn't help but notice that Anne's comfortable cardigan had several signs of wear and tear in it. I think it may have been her contribution to the role of an English eccentric.

Suitably nourished we said our goodbyes to Anne and Tim before heading down the delightful driveway, with its circular flower border half way along incorporating a sun dial atop a plinth and large lawns to either side, with trees shrouding the broad gates that led to the road. I couldn't help wishing I'd been born and raised in a house like The Old Rectory.

As we headed up a back lane towards Nether Row, with the sun already beaming down on us, the surrounding scenery was becoming classic Lakeland territory. None was more so than the

Caldbeck Fells directly in front of us, at 658 metres: the highest point of our entire walk. The summit, known as High Pike, is one of the 214 listed Wainwrights in the Lake District. These gain their name from Alfred Wainwright, immortal in the walking world for his magical seven book series "The Pictorial Guides to the Lakeland Fells". They were his 13-year labour of love between 1952 and 1965, all hand written, and hand illustrated in magnificent detail. Walkers aim to reach the summit of all 214 Wainwrights over time and this was to be our 89th success.

After gently rising until reaching Nether Row, our path necessarily took on a steep ascent up through tussocky grass for the 1.5-mile stint to the top. We knew it would be tough, but our logic in planning today's mountainous route was to do this climb at the start of the walk while we were still relatively fresh. It was already proving hot work in the strong morning sun, which in burning off yesterday's rain was creating a hazy day, but the visibility for high level walking was still good. Half way up the path strangely disappeared and with no summit visible at that point, it was time to use the compass to keep us on course. By following the literal line of the compass, we endured 30 minutes of climbing across very uneven, thick tussocks, often with ground-hugging gorse and the occasional hidden dyke, which really sapped a lot of energy out of our legs.

The ground finally improved and we victoriously reached the summit cairn to take the mandatory 'selfie' with our mobile phone. The descent from there towards Grainsgill Beck was much more straightforward, though the narrow path tracking the cascading beck down 200 metres in height was rocky and arduous, with progress very slow at times. As we reached the next turning point at 5.5 miles we'd already been walking for nearly 4 hours. It was going to be a long day in more than just mileage. Thankfully the next path was a broad track, very easy to walk on, enabling us to claw back some of the time lost as we headed for

Skiddaw House, a Youth Hostel Association establishment at our 9 miles point. Along this stretch we had the so far unusual experience of crossing paths with other walkers as they headed north on their Cumbria Way challenge.

The track continued to be good from Skiddaw House, as we passed under the crags of Lonscale Fell with views east towards Blencathra. At 12 miles, we got our first views of Keswick and the instantly recognisable Derwent Water, with the impressive Catbells range standing guard over its western bank. The weather continued to be humid and hazy and it came as no surprise to hear a few rumbles of thunder. We knew that rain was forecast for later, but we had the distinct feeling we were heading for a repeat of yesterday's wet ending to the day.

As we crossed the footbridge over the busy A66, we tried to pick up the pace again as the first drops of rain arrived. There was less than a mile to go to our B&B, Birch How, which was situated on the east side of town. The rain became heavier and annoyingly, we had to resort to our waterproofs for the final 10 minutes of walking.

We located the Victorian Brundholme Terrace, with its traditional grey Lakeland slate roofs and walls, just beyond Fitz Park, with Birch House mid-way along. Our host Carolyn opened the door to us and I immediately spotted that Maureen's rucksack had arrived okay. It had been a long day, but after freshening up we had sufficiently recovered to take a stroll into Keswick for a well-earned dinner at an Italian cafe bar close to the Moot Hall.

The next morning, we awoke knowing that this was one of our so-called rest days. Our walk today would be a 7.5 miles meander to the village of Rosthwaite, located in the beautiful Borrowdale beyond the far end of Derwent water. But before then we effectively had the morning off. Carolyn kindly let us leave our walking gear and rucksacks in the B&B until midday and even gave us a key for when we returned as she needed to go out. After breakfast, we took the short walk into the town centre where Maureen had booked herself into a hairdresser. I took the opportunity to look around the many walking gear shops to suss out any bargains. Maureen emerged from the salon duly trimmed and styled, following which we visited the Keswick branch of our favourite store, Cotswolds Outdoors, and both bought a few replacement tops and socks (i.e. no net increase in items in our rucksacks!), before heading back to the B&B to collect our things.

It was just after noon when we eventually got underway, heading out of the west side of town to reach Portinscale where we re-joined the Cumbria Way, surrounded by impressive mountains. A quiet lane led to a footpath through woods until it dropped down to the water's edge just after Hawes End. Just like the sun on the water, we reflected on this being our first contact with a lake since entering the Lake District. Throughout Scotland most such expanses of water are lochs, but as soon as the border is crossed the word becomes lake, meaning the same. The conundrum though is that there is only one stretch of water named 'lake' in the Lake District and it isn't the one we were now admiring. Bassenthwaite Lake, a few miles to the north-west of Derwent Water, has that accolade. Some suggest that's why this region is called The Lake (singular) District, whilst also being generally referred to as the Lakes or Lakeland.

After another hot, sunny start to the day the sky clouded over, but it remained quite humid. The wooded path clung to the edge of the lake for a couple of miles, the calm water lapping onto the shingle shoreline. Strangely, walkers coming towards us were noticeably wet and told us of heavy showers at Grange, just up ahead. Almost inevitably we caught up with it and reluctantly put on our waterproofs again. Just like the previous two days around this time, the heavens opened big time. We marched along the now sodden footpath to reach the lane to Grange, but the rain was ridiculously heavy, so we took shelter in a roadside wood store.

It was all a bit unreal, sitting on freshly chopped logs intended for the Borrowdale Gates Hotel, whose store we had invaded. When the rain eased ever so slightly we opted to dash for it, intending to find the coffee shop we knew was in Grange. But the Rain God spotted us and threw everything at us again, so we scampered down the hotel's drive and leapt into their outer porch.

"Come in, don't worry about being wet", said the receptionist from the sanctuary of her dry desk. "Hang your waterproofs behind the door to your left and feel free to go through to the lounge area", she advised. This seemed equally unreal, here in the reception area of a 4-star hotel, soaked and dripping wet, being welcomed like paying guests on a summer's day. We did as we were instructed, took our wet gear and boots off and gingerly stepped through to the lounge. 10 minutes later we were eating scones, teacakes and drinking coffee looking out on the rain we'd just escaped from bouncing on the patio furniture outside the lounge windows!

Half an hour passed by before the rain stopped. We returned to reception, paid our bill, thanked them profusely for their amazing hospitality and stuffed our wet gear under the straps of our rucksacks, in the vain hope that they might dry off as we walked. We had just 1.5 miles to go on lanes in what was now a lovely, sunny end to the day, and soon found Yew Tree Farm, our B&B for the night, on the outskirts of Rosthwaite.

The warm weather continued the next morning, with the outlook promising for a dry day, all day – nothing in the forecast to suggest an end of day soaking, like on the previous three days! We left Rosthwaite still on the Cumbria Way as it sidled up alongside Stonethwaite Beck for the first 1.5 miles. A local farmer was using his excellent collie dogs to round up and pen his flock of Herdwick sheep, which are native to the Lake District. Today we'd be wrapped up in classic Lakeland mountains and valleys on our 12.5 miles walk to Ambleside. A right turn took us into a wide valley with Langstrath Beck, now our companion, the towering Borrowdale Fell to our right and High Raise to our left. As we reached the 3 mile point our hard climb for the day was clear for us to see. The path for the 250 metres climb up to Stake Pass zigzagged from the valley bottom to the discernible top, taking some of the steepness out of the climb but doubling the distance needed to get there. It was hard going nonetheless and very time consuming. Our day just got longer in distance and time on our legs.

At last the path levelled out and we were now in the land of the giants. Ahead of us was Crinkle Crags, to our left the Langdale Pikes and to our right the daddy of them all, Scafell Pike, all 978 metres of it and the tallest mountain in England. As dramatic and awe inspiring as Scafell Pike is, it made me realise even more as I looked across at it just how monstrous Scotland's Munro mountains are in comparison. Scafell Pike is one of only 4 'Wainwrights' that would qualify by height to be a Munro and it would be 175th on the list in height order!

Almost instantly the path started its descent under the rocky slopes of Langdale Fell before levelling out in the valley below, where at 7 miles we stopped for a break at the delightful Old Dungeon Ghyll Hotel. We were surprisingly weary, with plenty of walking still to do.

The fantastic scenery continued as we joined the Great Langdale valley. The weather really does make or break the Lake District and today it was very much in our favour. The sun intermixed with passing clouds, gave the mountain sides a rich texture and were stunning to gaze at. Soon we were heading into Elterwater and it was here that we ended our association with the

Cumbria Way. While it headed due south on its journey to Ulverston, we now needed to take an easterly course for a few days to take us out of the Lakes and into Lancashire. A mile of lane walking led us to Loughrigg Tarn, a quiet secluded circle of water in which a couple of swimmers were enjoying a no-doubt invigorating experience.

I could see that Maureen was hot, bothered and flagging now and she would probably have opted for joining the swimmers, given the choice, and calling it a day. But there were still 2 miles to go to reach Ambleside, which unfortunately involved a stiff climb away from the tarn up the side of Ivy Crag. It was a good path but hard underfoot. "I can't do much more today, I'm done for", she said. It seemed to be taking an age for Ambleside to come into view and my chances of pacifying her were slim. "I'm sure it's just over the next rise and then downhill into town. Keep going", I said in an upbeat tone. I took over her rucksack for the final assault and then there it was. Thankfully I'd booked a B&B on this west side of town.

It had been a great day's walk, but a tiring one. The Lakes were proving a tough re-introduction to walking in England after the relatively flat terrain of the Scottish border region. As well as a comfortable B&B in the centre of town, the prize at the end of the day I'd most been looking forward to, was our evening meal. A long-time favourite eating place of ours in Ambleside is the Jade Garden Chinese restaurant, which just happened to be 4 doors down from our B&B, Claremont House. After freshening up we eased ourselves along the pavement to enjoy a wonderful meal there. And to top it off, I followed this up with another favourite, a rum and raisin ice cream on the way back to our room.

The next morning did not begin well for many reasons. When I asked Maureen how she was feeling she replied, "My back's aching and I feel worn out". I was starting to become worried that this walk was taking more out of her than expected. She was used to long distance walking, but we hadn't done one of this duration for 4 years. That's plenty of time for both our bodies to become less resilient and perhaps take more time to recover from the tougher days. For myself I felt pretty good so far. I'd no aches or pains to speak of and I knew that if I eased my legs into the day from the moment I dropped them over the side of the bed I should be okay.

I drew open the curtains to reveal a mizzy day outside. Mist hung over the nearby hills and there was a faint drizzle of rain, one of those that have a habit of soaking you wet without you realising it. A 12.5 mile walk to Kendal faced us, not the longest of days and not expected to be too arduous. We set off shortly after 9am to head south-east on a footpath heading for Skelghyll Wood, with early elevated views over the mist covered Windermere water. Later that day an annual swim in Windermere would be taking place, when some 15,000 swimmers would be taking to the chilling water. An unexpectedly steep climb through the wood followed. "I thought you said this would be a short uphill bit, not half way up Everest", Maureen bemoaned. She wasn't happy. Thankfully it levelled off and remained largely so until we reached Town End, at just less than 3 miles.

After crossing the road, we stopped to read a sign at the end of our intended path, which stated "Footbridge closed. Proceed with caution". We decided it was still okay to go forward and followed the path downhill to see what the situation was at Trout Beck. The footbridge wasn't just closed, it was completely wrecked by floods and couldn't be used. As there was no alternative way of crossing the fast-flowing beck, we evidently couldn't "proceed with caution", in fact not at all. We had no choice but to take the steep walk back up the footpath to the road. All in all, we'd wasted 20 minutes and some precious energy.

"I'll be emailing Cumbria County Council about this tonight. Why not simply say 'no through route – bridge down'", Maureen said, angrily. She was still unhappy. "Now which way do we go", she demanded, seeking an instant solution to our dilemma. I looked at the map and found there wasn't another crossing without heading quite some way north, which wasn't an option. The only thing to do was lane-walk south until we reached the A591 at Troutbeck Bridge, which would still take us some 4 miles off our intended route. Fortunately, the lane didn't see much traffic and it was mostly downhill, but the biggest frustration was that we weren't making any progress east. Once at the A591 we still had 9 miles to go. I then made Maureen an offer, both to help the situation and try to improve her mood.

"Given that we've walked 4 miles out of our way, I can justify us catching a bus to take us 4 miles on to Staveley", I suggested. "What do you think?"

"I think it makes sense if you don't feel bad at not walking it", she replied.

"I wouldn't do it if we gained miles by using a bus, but as it's the same difference I'm okay with it", I said.

After 10 minutes sat on the nearby bench, bus 555 came to our assistance. It had been several years since I last caught a bus, so it was a novel experience to do so again. Many people got on at Windermere Station. One lady sat on the seats in front of ours and almost immediately turned around and started chatting to us. She told us her name was Faith and that she moved to the area 2 years ago. She also advised us to go for a coffee at the Cafe Eclec in Staveley. We thanked her as we rose to get off and duly went there for lunch.

By the end of lunch Maureen had calmed down, she was suitably replenished and felt committed to finishing the day's walk. That said a call from home regarding one of our granddaughters did give her cause for concern and left her feeling even more homesick than she already was. She had to dig deep to continue as the pull from home was very strong.

After a short distance of lane walking out of Staveley we turned onto a footpath. The surrounding scenery was much gentler now, signifying the start of our exit from the Lake District mountain region. Some 3 miles on we passed through the village of Burnside. We couldn't help but notice the local bus shelter, which must surely qualify as one of the best kept in Britain. It was brick built and painted over white, with a grey roof. The inside was a reddish-brown colour, with a bench to sit on and an information board which included a bus timetable. Interestingly the large front window and the two side windows were double glazed, even though the entrance was an open arch rather than a door. I guess someone must have had the double-glazing panes going spare at some point! There was a window box on one side festooned with flowering plants and the grass area around the shelter was neatly cut. It was great to see some local pride in action.

Soon afterwards we entered the outskirts of Kendal. The road traffic was getting progressively busier as we reached the town centre around 4.30pm. We checked into our B&B, the Shakespeare Inn, and were grateful to reach our room and flop onto the bed. It had been a strange, disjointed and challenging day. Maureen was out on her feet. "I'm seriously thinking I can't walk again tomorrow", Maureen said "I might have to take a proper rest day. I'm absolutely exhausted". I was very concerned. When Maureen uses the word 'exhausted' that's what she is, not just tired or weary but genuinely and completely whacked. Tomorrow would be a long one, with 17.5 miles to walk. I sat on the edge of the bed contemplating possible options, as Maureen drifted into a deep sleep.

Chapter 7 – Witch Way Next?

"Morning babe. Good news", I said as Maureen was stirring. "I've booked a taxi to take your rucksack to Kirkby Lonsdale. It'll be here at 8.30am. If you want a day off I can get it to come this afternoon while you have the morning in Kendal. You could then go with the taxi and I'll see you later".

"A day without a rucksack and you having a lighter one will be great. I'm going to do the walk", Maureen said. Her fortitude is amazing. If I'd felt like she did at the end of yesterday I know I couldn't have walked again today, even after a good night's sleep.

"That's brilliant, if you're sure", I said. We'd got 17.5 miles to do, but the first 12 miles were due to be as flat as a proverbial pancake. There's a climb between 12 and 14 miles and then generally flat again until the end.

We had just finished breakfast when the taxi driver poked his head through the door. "Taxi for Mr Shipley", he announced. We walked over to greet him. "It's just this rucksack to go, mate", I said to his obvious surprise. "The owner of the Copper Kettle B&B is expecting you, but please ensure you hand this to her rather than just leave it and could you text me when it's safely delivered please". "Will do, no problem", he said and with that he was gone.

Just 25 minutes later, shortly just after we'd settled our bill and were heading out into the street, my mobile bleeped to show a short message saying, "Bag delivered okay". Our rucksack was at Kirkby Lonsdale already, but for us it would take the best part of 9 hours to walk the same distance!

There was a very light drizzle of rain as we walked up the High Street, but we chanced starting off in shorts and lightweight tops. Heading due south for the first 10 miles, we soon picked up our footpath to Natland. Just as we did the heavens opened, so it was on with our waterproofs, which we'd stay in for the remainder of the day. The path crossed a series of fields progressively heading towards a herd of Holsteins directly on our route. Being in no mood in the wet weather to encounter cows, we redirected onto lanes until Natland and continued in the same vein to the next village of Sedgwick, before passing through the pleasant Levens Deer Park.

Overall the scenery here was very flat and gentle countryside. We were now only a geographical stone's throw from Morecambe Bay. This could have featured in our walk, as an early version of the route would have seen us reach nearby Ulverston by completing the whole of the Cumbria Way and then crossing the bay. However, Morecambe Bay is notorious for its quicksand and fast-moving tides (it is said that the tide can come in "as fast as a horse can run"). On the night of 5th February 2004, 23 Chinese immigrant cockle pickers drowned after being cut off by the tides. Crossing the bay can only be undertaken at specified times and by following an experienced guide. This all sounded too problematic, too dangerous and was taking us out of our way. The alternative would have been to take a large loop north-east from Ulverston to get around the bay. Neither option appealed to me, so I re-designed the route to go east to Kendal and then on to Kirkby Lonsdale, avoiding Morecambe Bay altogether.

At 8 miles, we came to Milnthorpe, the only option on today's route to stop for lunch. There were several cafes and pubs around the town centre and we opted, for no reason, to try the Cross Keys Inn. As we walked into the public bar, sitting there similarly taking a break was none other than Faith, who we met on the bus yesterday. "Wow, this is a coincidence", I said to her. She was in Milnthorpe to collect a parcel, before catching another bus home. We joined her for lunch, following which we went our separate ways. This had been our second 'small world' scenario, the other being Dave at the B&B in Kirkcaldy who worked in the same building as we had done at Rolls-Royce in Derby. I felt sure there'd be at least one more such experience before we reached Dover. What I didn't anticipate was that it would be later the same day!

Outside it was still raining quite heavily, leading us to resume lane walking until we reached our intended bridge over the M6. Crossing this motorway felt like a shift from the west side of the country to the middle 'block' that sits between the M6 and the A1 to the east. We wouldn't be venturing too far into middle England however, before we would cross back to the west in a few days' time. Our immediate course would take us due east for the remainder of the day, initially rising along the side of Holmepark Fell and across the lower slopes of Hutton Roof Crags. These were our first hills of any note for quite a while and they were covered in a dense rolling mist. We reached Hutton Roof village without any problems though and then continued to today's destination.

Kirkby Lonsdale sits in the south-east corner of Cumbria, marking our last port of call in the region. Tomorrow we'd cross into Lancashire, something we were both looking forward to as we'd done very little walking there previously. We made our way to the centre of this small town where our intriguing B&B, the Copper Kettle, was located. Our hosts, Pam and Peter, had seemingly been running their business for nigh on 40 years, so we reckoned they must be well into retirement age by now. The online reviews were very mixed, with visitors either finding the place quirky and comfortable or outdated and tired looking. I don't judge too much from reviews, but in this instance, they were very divided, either very pro or very 'never again' in their comments, with virtually none in between. I was also intrigued how they could offer two three-course evening meals for the princely sum of £10 each!

Pam opened the door to us and gave us the essential warm welcome. The first room serves as a cafe during the day, with a bar at the end for drinks in the evening. Pam led us up the challenging, narrow and near vertical stairs to our room. It was homely but, as some previous visitors had described, clearly hadn't been updated for several decades. The electrics were old, bulky switches with wires climbing the walls and running around the picture pelmet to unknown destinations. After freshening up we went down for the bargain dinner, hoping we wouldn't still be hungry afterwards. Peter, who we'd not seen earlier, appeared from the kitchen and looked a bit of a character. He had a strong Midlands accent and sported a bandana, which was evidently his choice of chef's headgear while he cooked. He explained that he was a cook on ocean liners for many years before starting the B&B.

Then came 'small world' incident number 2 of the day.

"Where do you come from Peter?" I asked.

"I'm originally from Leicestershire", he replied.

"I have relatives in that area. Where about in Leicestershire were you?" I enquired.

"You won't have heard of it", he said, "It's a small village called Fleckney".

"That's where my relatives are from and they still live there", I said.

"I lived on Albert Road at number 8", he said.

"My auntie and a cousin lived on that road at numbers 2 and 2A", I said. "What an unbelievable coincidence!"

116

As it turned out he didn't know any of my relatives when I went into their details, but it was still amazing that he should have lived on the very same road as they did.

The evening meal was lovely, with a starter of egg mayonnaise, steak and kidney pie for my main course (beef and vegetables for Maureen) and treacle sponge pudding with lashings of custard for dessert. We accompanied this with drinks to toast our success at having near-as-damn-it reached 500 miles, with just half a mile left to do first thing in the morning. Tomorrow would also be day 39, the halfway point of our Caper in terms of walking days. Just as we were thinking of calling it a day, Pam had a word with us.

"There's an England football match on the telly at the pub next door tonight. It might get a bit rowdy later. I've also got six people coming in late after a wedding reception, who may also be a bit noisy if they've had a few", she said. "So, I've got these eye masks and ear plugs if you wanted to use them", she continued. And with that she handed us each a small unopened package, in a style that suggested she might have been an air stewardess once upon a time (an airline may also have been where they came from). Unable to refuse for laughing, we just said "Great, many thanks Pam". Maureen made use of them!

We opened the curtains to Sunday 12th June 2016 and the prospect of a 'rest day', walking 8.5 miles to Hornby. The boy in me immediately thought of model trains, but alas Hornby village has no connection with the company that bears its name. Our route would follow the Lune Valley Ramble due south, tracking the River Lune most of the way. The contour lines would stick to very modest 30 metres above sea level, with hardly an incline in sight all day. To complete the picture of an easy, pleasant day ahead the weather forecast was for a dry, sunny day.

After leaving the Copper Kettle a short stroll through the back lanes of Kirkby Lonsdale brought us to Devil's Bridge. The peace and tranquillity of the Sunday morning was being temporarily shattered by an ever-increasing number of motorbikes, who evidently gather at this Hell's Angels alter before setting off on their group ride.

Our path dropped down from the bridge to the riverside and into Lancashire. Immediately next to the stile was a small herd of cows, sat motionless except for chewing the cud, who kindly let us pass with hardly a glance in our direction. It was easy walking through numerous pastures for 5 miles, until the next pasture caused us to check our map for alternatives. It was a huge expanse of grass, with an equally huge herd of cows in the distance. They may well have been just as benevolent as their mates back down the river, but if they weren't there was nowhere to escape for at least 300 yards. Not the kind of scenario we like and not worth the risk when a quiet country lane nearby would take us to Arkholme hassle free. It was coming up to midday when we reached the village and being too nice a day to rush things we opted for coffees and cake at the local pub, which we enjoyed sitting outside under a sun canopy.

Replenished, we returned to the riverside path. A couple of easy miles ensued through more pastures, and a pleasant wood, that took us to Loyn Bridge just as a light rain shower fell. Soon afterwards we were entering Hornby. It was still relatively early, so we had an early snack in the local cafe, which doubles as the Post Office, while the rain passed through...it can be tough at times on these walks! Around 4pm we set off for our accommodation, Whitmoor Vegetarian B&B, on the east side of the town. It was the only accommodation in the area. I'd judged that it wouldn't be an issue to have a lighter, meat-free breakfast in the morning for once and it may even do our digestive systems some good.

Our hosts, Rita and Keith, had built Whitmore to their own design in 1995 using recycled sandstone from an old barn. It was clear when we walked in that they were into all things natural, with oak flooring, beams and staircase, a log burner, lots of natural wood furniture and a very rustic looking house. Our room was a delight, being split level with a large sofa on the raised element, overlooking their picture book garden, which was full of colour. Rita and Keith were interesting people. Keith had an image like a well-travelled explorer, whilst Rita was more of a disciple of Glastonbury. They were very welcoming and made us instantly feel at home. The vegetarian aspect meant no coffee on offer, but rather a variety of oddly flavoured teas. As neither of us are tea drinkers we opted to use our illicit supply of coffee sachets gathered from earlier B&B's and covertly broke the rules in the seclusion of our room.

At times like these we do consider ourselves very lucky to stay in such comfortable places as opposed to using a tent. The down side of course is the cost and at an average of £75 per night, the overall costs of this 78-day walk were significant. But it's how we chose to do it and it took many years of saving to raise the necessary funds.

After a very organic, though lovely breakfast, we set off back to the village to visit the Post Office. We had a few items of clothing in our rucksacks that we weren't making any use of and several OS maps which were no-longer needed, so it made sense whilst there was a Post Office handy to send them home rather than carry them. In this respect, if there's one sight we saw every day on this walk, regardless of how remote a part of the UK we were in, it was the red van of Postman Pat. All hail to the Royal Mail and may this great British institution be defended and preserved whenever its existence comes under threat.

Our packages securely in the post we set off for the moors and our 13.5 mile walk to Slaidburn. The first couple of miles were a steady climb out of Hornby, followed by a long descent to Barkin Bridge at 3 miles. We took a short bags-off break here as we knew the next 6 miles would be continuously uphill onto the exposed moors, rising to a summit point at 416 metres. Good weather would have been ideal, but as we humped our rucksacks back on the sky ahead gave out a grim message – we were soon going to get very wet! The sky grew darker and more dramatic as we marched on, hoping that we'd somehow escape the inevitable soaking. Maybe it was because we were heading towards the 'land of the witches', but it seemed quite sinister and bleak up on the moors. The sky to our right was jet black and heading towards us. We danced with the devil lurking within them for 3 more miles before the torrent began and our waterproofs were needed. Vertical shafts of rain battered us as we climbed ever higher, fortunately on a clear track and a good surface.

Despite this pummelling, the fells were impressive if foreboding, and we could imagine that on a dry, sunny day the landscape would have provided great views. At 9 miles, the summit was reached, and it was all downhill from there. Within a short distance the rain had stopped, the skies brightened and slowly our sodden gear began to dry a little as we continued along Salter Fell. We were now in the Forest of Bowland, though trees were quite sparse at this point. Aside the track we came across a large white stone block with the inscription 'Witches 400'. This is a memorial stone laid in 2012 to one of the so-called Lancashire Witches, marking the 400th anniversary of them being burnt at the stake.

The track led onto a lane and took us down into Slaidburn where our land-locked accommodation, Hark to Bounty Inn, stood waiting for us. The inn oozed with character on the outside and once indoors we were met with low ceilings, dark beams, lots of wooden furniture and a large open fireplace. It is reputed to date back to the 1300s and was known as The Dog until 1875. Apparently, the squire of the village, who was also the Rector, dropped in with his hunting mates for a few drinks, leaving the pack of dogs tied up outside. The story goes that high above the noise of the other hounds could be heard the squire's favourite dog, which prompted him to call out "Hark to Bounty!" Nothing nautical about the inn's name after all. Seemingly the landlord at the time was so impressed by the squire's outburst that he changed the inn's name! Perhaps if this event was repeated in modern times the inn would become "Quiet, damn you!"

We were warmly greeted and shown to our room which, unlike the public area downstairs, was decorated in a very modern way. It was suggested that we put our wet coats and over trousers to dry in the Courtroom, a huge high ceilinged upstairs room spanning the length of the inn, which was used as the local court from the early 19th century until the mid-1930s. You could sense the history of the place and easily imagine what would have taken place there all those years ago.

That evening, between dinner courses in the bar, Maureen checked our sponsorship website. We were delighted to discover that, through the generosity of many, many people, we had reached our target of £1,041. We naturally had a celebratory drink to this success on behalf of all our sponsors!

A light breakfast was in order the next morning, after the previous evening's hearty Lancashire meal, then it was rucksacks on to get day 41 underway. Ahead lay a relatively short day of 10 miles that would take us to a place where I particularly wanted to stay, Angram Green Farm on the outskirts of Downham. The farm sits snugly at the very foot of Pendle Hill, a key 'must-do' I'd planned as part of this journey. After a steady climb for the first mile through several pastures, our route became quite steep for the next 2 miles before levelling out on the moor at 368 metres, curiously marked on the OS map as 'The Wife (pile of stones)'. It was easy walking thereafter, along a clear path with open views of the surrounding countryside. The weather was being kinder today, no sun to speak of but dry all the same.

After 8 miles, we reached the small town of Chatburn where we stopped to speak to a local chap who was doing a spot of gardening. Downham's claim to fame is that the 1961 film 'Whistle Down the Wind', starring the wonderful Hayley Mills, was filmed at a local farm. The story line surrounded Hayley's character, Kathy Bostock, and her young siblings who jump to the conclusion that the man they find in their barn, an escaped killer, is none other than Jesus Christ. I'd designed the route to pass by the farm, so we could look.

"Do you know if there's much to see at Worsaw End Farm?", I asked the gardener.

"You mean the place where they filmed 'Whistle Down the Wind', nothing there at all", he said. "There's not even a sign mentioning it outside, it's just a normal working farm now. I wouldn't make a special trip to go there, if I were you", he said.

Well, that took the 'wind' out of my sails, so to speak. I don't know what I was expecting to find there now, some 55 years after the film was made, but I imagined there would be something.

"No point wasting our energies if we can get to our B&B more directly", Maureen suggested. She was aware what was awaiting us the next morning. A quick check on the OS map found a couple of paths and a lane that would lead us to Angram Green Farm, so we re-routed the last 2 miles. As we approached the farm Pendle Hill came increasingly into view. It lay in the valley like a giant whale, long and rounded with steep sloping sides. At 557 metres, it stands head and shoulders above nearby lesser mortals, who top no more than 430 metres. Once in our B&B we kept looking at it through the window of our room, excited at the prospect of scaling its heights.

After a good night's sleep and an early breakfast, we headed out on a path passing behind the farm. The first 300 metres were flat, but then a sharp right turn meant only one thing...up we go. We were now on the Witches Way, a 48-mile journey from Sabden in Lancashire heading through the Ribble Valley and the Forest of Bowland to Lancaster. It would be our route south-east for the first 8 miles of our 12.5 miles to Worsthorne on the far side of Burnley. Within no time we were gaining good height, with great views opening back in the direction of where we'd walked over the last few days. It was tough going but, as with High Pike in the Lake District, the theory was to do this first while we were reasonably fresh. It didn't stop us breathing heavily as we climbed, reaching the first of two major cairns after an hour's uphill walking.

The cairn was a good 10 feet tall, shaped like a thimble and constructed of slate bricks. It bore an inscription stating it was dedicated by the Scout movement. Although Pendle Hill is prone to being shrouded in mist, today it was totally clear. This made following the well-trodden path easy as we navigated our way across the flat top through a sea of wild cotton plants, swaying in the gentle breeze. The second cairn was soon reached, this one a storm shelter with no roof, but walls 5 feet high that would certainly shelter walkers from the strong winds that can whip up there.

Across a ladder stile and 400 yards further on we reached the summit trig point. Fantastic 360-degree views from there, with the sprawling town of Burnley nestled in the valley over the east side of the hill. There were several other walkers enjoying this popular monolith, including a guy who kindly took the standard photo of us at the summit. In chatting with him we learned that he was still doing plenty of walking, including summit climbs like today, despite having had two hip replacements. Respect!

A long, snaking descent led us into the small village of Barley, one of several nearby villages reputedly where witches lived and cast their spells. We stopped at the local tea rooms for a well-earned coffee. A group of local men, their ruddy complexions suggesting a life of many years working the surrounding hills, were challenging each other as to which is best, Lancashire or Yorkshire. It could have escalated into another War of the Roses, but it remained good humoured while we were there and was continuing as we left.

The route then doubled up with the Pendle Way as we made our way across pleasant pastures, abundant with wild flowers. Progress downhill was good as we briefly joined a riverside path before turning off to head for a bridge over the M65. It never ceases to surprise me how peace and tranquillity can so quickly become motorway madness and noise, but equally a few minutes beyond the bridge it was quiet again. At the Leeds and Liverpool Canal we joined the Bronte Way to circumnavigate the outskirts of Burnley. As the canal side path took us past some large former mills, the sound of a light aircraft could be heard above. We looked skywards to see it had a banner in tow which read 'Vote Leave', a reference to the forthcoming European Union Referendum on 23rd June, just over a week away.

I totally missed a connecting path to the River Bran, causing us to go out of our way by about a mile. Tiredness was setting in by now, so I suggested we lane walked the remainder to Worsthorne. It was one of those occasions when it seemed like an eternity until we got there, and it was proving hard to appease Maureen, who openly admits to getting irritable when she's tired.

We eventually reached the village around 5.45pm and located our B&B, simply called The Guest House. Our host dropped by and advised us that there was nowhere to eat in the village, despite it having two pubs, and that the local fish and chip shop would shut at 6pm. We hurriedly got to it just in time and, with it being a pleasant evening, sat outside to eat a classic cod and chips.

We returned to the B&B to empty our rucksacks and freshen up. Now, we've stayed in some strange places over the years but this one takes some beating. Firstly, on entering from the street you're in a shared lounge. Nothing wrong with that, except that it had little in the way of furniture and had a cold, hardwood floor, making it altogether uninviting. The weird thing though was the CCTV camera into the room. It implied that the owner would be watching and recording everything his guests did in there. It was suggested that this was for our security, but it's the first time I've ever come across inward facing CCTV cameras.

Access to our room was by entering a four-digit code into a lock, not what you'd expect in a village B&B. Strategically placed on the bed where we wouldn't miss it was what can only be described as the rules and regulations for staying there, certainly not a welcome brochure. There were numerous 'do's and don'ts', including not making marks on any of the furniture or bed linen or a fine would be imposed! It read like someone who didn't really want you to do anything much beyond breathing.

As the B&B didn't have its own dining facilities, we'd been advised that breakfast the next morning would be taken at the cafe next door, but when we went there a little after 8.00am it was closed. We peered through the window and could see that there was someone in a room to the rear, so we knocked hard on the door to gain their attention. When a lady answered the door, she said that she hadn't been told there were guests in the B&B.

Normally the cafe didn't open to the public until 10.00am. However, she was considerably more accommodating than our host, ushering us in and rustling up a nice breakfast.

As we ate we were excited by the prospect of soon being joined by Frances Ipson, another of our virtual friends from the Country Walking Facebook Group, who we'd be meeting for the first time. Frances lives in nearby Bradford and had been in touch to offer us a rucksack transfer to today's destination of Hollingworth Lake, some 14 miles away. Just as we were finishing breakfast the cafe door opened and she was here, a beaming smile instantly recognisable from many online photos. We gave each other a hug like long-time friends meeting up again. Frances joined us for a coffee, over which walking was the only topic of conversation, as you might expect, before we all made our way outside. We handed over Maureen's rucksack and then she was gone, with neither of us knowing when our paths were likely to cross again. It's a very welcome but strange feeling when you meet someone in person that you've only ever known online, have a short period in the land of 'reality' and then part again, our next contact inevitably back in the 'virtual' world of Facebook.

Today's walk would be a solid trek through the Lancashire countryside, one we were looking forward to really experience this area and make a judgement on its future walking potential. The walk started off okay with a short lane stretch out of Worsthorne to then pick up the Burnley Way. Our first hill climb of the day was a gentle affair, before the path dropped back down towards a farm. A couple of wire fences had been erected cutting off the right of way, resulting in two awkward climb overs before successfully reaching a road. Another short climb ensued onto the moors, where the path levelled off to give wide ranging views back towards Burnley.

At 3 miles, the way markers for the Burnley Way either disappeared or we missed a few, resulting in a difficult climb over hard terrain to reach Thieveley Point at 449 metres. The ground was quite churned up and muddy, but was reasonable to walk on until it became the Rossendale Way. The path deteriorated and was at times unclear, boot-deep in mud in places and several walk rounds needed at flooded points. A herd of cows had to be avoided, quickly followed by six very lively wild horses roaming close enough to us to cause concern, and then a section through farm buildings. To describe the farm as a disgusting dump would be putting it mildly! There was old machinery rusting in random places, the yards hadn't been swilled this century, the animals all looked in poor condition and the smell was indescribable. We passed through there as quickly as possible.

Further along we came to the next obstacle and it couldn't have been much bigger. Our path was on course to pass directly under a newly built wind turbine. There was no notice re-directing walkers and as we moved ever closer it became obvious that if we stuck to the path the tip of a turbine blade would part what little hair I still have on my head. We decided to sidle over a few hundred metres through rough ground to where a site track led to two further turbines, though it kept a safer distance from them. Here we picked up what I thought was our path again and continued this until just after 9 miles, when I realised we were off course and heading slightly westwards. As we topped Brown Wardle Hill I could see where we needed to be, rather than where we were. By this time Maureen was already frustrated by the trials of the day, but I bravely admitted that we'd gone wrong and plotted a revised route to get us back on track. This is one aspect of walking where we are very different. I don't like to go wrong, but I can accept that it's happened and sort it out. Maureen, especially after a hard day of walking, will be angry at wasting energy by going wrong when she's already tired and quite openly lets me know that she is! An argument inevitably ensues and as much as we both hit out at each other, we generally finish the walk okay and calm down later.

By now we'd crossed from Lancashire into the Greater Manchester region. After skirting Watergrove Reservoir we came upon the hamlet of Wardle, where we stopped at the local Spar for a well-earned coffee. From there it was 1.5 miles of lane walking to Hollingworth, most noted for the nearby large lake that takes its name. Our B&B, unfortunately located at the top of a steep hill, was a detached house probably built in the 1950's, with a short drive leading to the front door. We rang the bell and the lady owner, Chris, welcomed us and said that our room was in an annex at the bottom of the rear garden. She then said, strangely, "I'll just change my feet and I'll be with you". How often at the end of a long day have we and no doubt many other walkers wished they could do just that! Or imagine if you could change your feet every 500 miles. A round-the-world walk would then be a possibility!

Once Chris had slipped into her garden shoes she took us round the back to the annex. 'In the garden' was more literal than I'd imagined, as the annex was covered in greenery, with plants growing up the outer walls and tree branches hanging over the windows. Inside it was cosy enough, but it was like looking out from a greenhouse when I peered through the window. "As long as no garden animals join us in the night it should be okay", I reassured Maureen. After freshening up we ventured out for our evening meal to the lakeside pub, interestingly called 'The Beach', especially as the nearest one was at least 80 miles away. Hollingworth was turning out to be a bit weird, I thought.

We were up early the next morning, having survived the night marooned in the jungle. A quick breakfast in the main house and we were off. A long 17 miles hike to Padfield lay ahead of us, where we would be having dinner with a former manager of ours when we worked at Rolls-Royce. It would be a great tonic for Maureen to see a friendly face, having had mostly just mine to see for the last month and a half.

As we skirted clockwise around Hollingworth Lake, I sensed that we'd be unlikely to return here again. Our path crossed a couple of pastures and then dipped under the busy M62 before heading towards a plethora of reservoirs. We passed between Norman Hill and Piethorne Reservoirs, with Kitcliffe and Ogden Reservoirs to our right and Rooden Reservoir ahead of us. They won't run out of water in these parts in a hurry!

A steep climb followed which eventually reached the A672, which we followed downhill into Denshaw. On the way down the road we came upon a coned off area, where two telecommunications workers were installing some underground cabling. The larger of them was half in a manhole facing away from us, with his jeans unfortunately worn at the traditional level of only half covering his hind quarters, revealing a significant amount of bare skin. His taller, thinner colleague was behind him, also facing away from us. They were attempting to insert a broad yellow tube into the manhole, which would subsequently contain cables. To say they were working it in together is probably underselling it, as they were rhythmically thrusting the tube inches at a time into the hole in complete unison. It didn't look altogether decent, but it was proving effective and it certainly made us smile!

The next 6 miles followed the Tame Valley Way, meandering through riverside pastures full of wild flowers, passing through Delph and Uppermill before reaching the hamlet of Greenfield. It was good to get some straight forward walking done, as we knew the final 6 miles would be hard going. Our route now joined the Pennine Bridleway, providing a good track as we bypassed Mossley at 13 miles. The Tame Valley had been a series of industrial style towns, plenty of traditional housing, old mills and factory buildings and a prominent church centrally located in each one. Now we needed to get over to Longdendale. A flatter option would have been to stay on the bridleway for the next 2 miles, but I'd planned to save a mile by going up and over the hillside, then drop to the two Swinshaw Reservoirs.

As we climbed up the narrow path the bracken became extremely thick, such that we had to push our legs through it rather than walk. It was a prickly mass of gorse and bracken, which took every opportunity to scratch any exposed skin that came its way. With much cursing and effort, we made it to the summit, then caught our breath before we descended to the reservoirs. We re-joined the Pennine Bridleway for easier last 2 miles to Hadfield, though even its pretentious undulations were telling on our now tired legs. After 44 days of walking we were now in our home county of Derbyshire. We'd dipped over the 'border' from Greater Manchester just as we reached Hadfield.

"How much further?", Maureen asked, coded talk for 'I've had enough for today and the B&B had better be around the next corner, Martin'. I knew it wasn't as there was still a mile to go to the almost identically named Padfield. What I didn't know was that it was all uphill. The route planner's skills were now being questioned by his companion, along with statements such as "I can't walk anymore". I tried to counter these with "Not far now, babe, up to the top, turn right and we'll be there". At times like these a mile seems to take forever, especially when we're in some new location and unfamiliar surroundings. We took a right and, hallelujah, there at last was our accommodation, The Peels Arms.

Rested and freshened up, we went down to dinner where our former colleague Simon Barker and his lovely wife Jacqui were waiting for us. Although he worked in Derby, Simon had always commuted from his home in Stalybridge, which is just a few miles down the road from Padfield. We had a great evening together and gained an unexpected bonus. Earlier when we first arrived we'd asked if they could possibly do a laundry wash for us. This was something we asked a B&B about every three days and in most cases, they'd agree, sometimes for a small charge, but not everyone would do it, as was the case here. We quite innocently mentioned this during idle conversation towards the end of our evening, at which point Jacqui instantly offered to do a wash for us and return it in the morning.

It had been a great get together with Simon and Jacqui. It gave us both a boost after so long without seeing a familiar face. Maureen felt encouraged by their support and taking the time to meet up with us. Being back in Derbyshire would lend itself to further visits by family and friends over the coming days, which should set us up nicely for the remaining 34 days of walking to reach Dover!

Chapter 8 – In Peak Conditions

It was Simon who did the honours with our freshly laundered clothing, dropping it off on route to his weekly Saturday morning round of golf. Kind support such as this really helps. And another such kindness quickly followed. No sooner had Simon left and breakfast was over, then Lindsay Pulley joined us. Lindsay is another fellow member of the Country Walking Facebook Group who had watched our progress down the UK and had been in touch to offer a baggage transfer service. We'd eagerly accepted and, as in previous instances, we piled all that we didn't need for the day into Maureen's rucksack, ready for Lindsay to take on to Whaley Bridge, 12 miles down the road.

Maureen was particularly grateful for the baggage transfer. The tough day yesterday had really taken it out of her and, despite a great night's sleep, she felt tired as we left the Peels Arms. Although not the longest of walks ahead of us, I did make some refinements to the route to make it more lane-based, which would be easier to walk on than the more arduous undulations of the open countryside. We headed down the road into the nearby town of Hadfield, quickly followed by passing through the fringes of Glossop and the hamlet of Charlesworth, before turning up a lane to endure our main climb of the day. I had been charged with finding a flat route to Whaley Bridge, but given that to get there we had to get over the hill that is Coombes Edge, it wasn't possible without a significant detour. So, the climb was inevitable. Despite this the trudge uphill was not, shall we say, appreciated!

Once at height, however, it was plain sailing. The weather was overcast but dry and a decent temperature. We remained on back lanes, with only the occasional car coming along to disturb the peace, until the welcome sight of the Pack Horse Inn greeted us just outside New Mills, with 9 miles completed. A light lunch was taken and then we were back on the road heading down to the Sett Valley Way.

The route here became unclear, with confusing signage, but we muddled our way through to move on to the Goyt Valley Way, which would be our companion until we reached Whaley Bridge. Most of this stretch was walked beside the Forest Canal, along which many stylish canal boats were moored. Birds were also plentiful, with a proud Heron dutifully positioned on the canal bank, ready to pounce on the first unsuspecting fish to come along, while a Mallard glided by pursued by her brood of twelve chicks.

Despite being from Derby, we hadn't previously spent a great deal of time in the Dark Peak Area, so today had been a new experience. We walked eagerly to the steps of today's accommodation, Springbank Guest House, where we were warmly met by our host. Susan is one of those wonderful B&B owners who have thought of everything and whatever you might want is right where you might need it most. Her place was an Aladdin's cave of all you need for a stay in complete comfort.

"Have our friends Julian and Wendy arrived?" I enquired.

"Yes, but I think they've popped into town for a few minutes," she said.

Julian and Wendy have been best friends of mine since our teenage years and whom Maureen had known since we first got together in 1998. They'd planned a weekend in the area to coincide with our arrival and would be walking with us the next day to Buxton. It would be great to see them as it would really give us both a boost, but especially Maureen. Being isolated on a walk of this nature is to be expected, but Maureen is someone who needs to see either friends or family on a regular basis. When she doesn't she's prone to feeling downhearted and however much I might cajole her, nothing beats meeting up with people dear to her heart.

After we'd freshened up I knocked on the door of their room and was greeted by Julian. "Hiya", he said as we shook hands, "You're looking good to say you've just walked 500-odd miles".

"Thanks", I said, as Wendy also came to the door. "I'm doing okay so far. Maureen's almost ready.

"I've booked us a table at a pub a few minutes' walk down the road", he said.

"Perfect, I could do with a walk", I joked.

We had a great evening catching up and I could see Maureen's spirits noticeably lifting, especially those in her glass! Well-fed and watered, we were all looking forward to our walk tomorrow, a 7.5 miles meander, and for Maureen and me one of our so-called 'rest' days.

As we left the B&B the next morning, we placed Maureen's rucksack into the boot of Julian's car, which was parked outside. He would be returning to collect his car after today's walk and would then drop the rucksack off at our B&B on their way home to Nottingham. Any respite from rucksack carrying was always welcome.

We set off and after just a few hundred yards we were back on our route. A narrow path took us down to the dam wall of Toddbrook Reservoir. Classic Derbyshire views along the length of the water and to the hills beyond were enhanced by another dry, warm day, ideal for walking. It had been a relief that good weather was forecast for our walk with friends. We've had days on other occasions when friends have met up with us and the weather has been atrocious. We would still do the walk because we were on a mission. Our friends would also feel obliged to accompany us, whether they truly wanted to or not, and we were very grateful for their support, but we always told them that opting out was okay and to drive to meet us at the other end...but they never did!

The path behind the dam led on to a pasture and a field gate at the far end, where a small group of Holstein cows were patiently waiting to greet us. We eased past them and thankfully they never motioned towards us. We were now on the Midshires Way for a short stretch, passing a couple of farms before entering Goyt Valley. The terrain was undulating but easy, straightforward walking.

As we progressed along the track we chatted as a foursome, rather than the more common divide of the 'guys' and the 'gals' that we and many other walkers often naturally veer towards. The talking habits of our respective genders are very different. Men usually catch up on the important issues in around ten minutes, then have periods of quiet whilst enjoying the walk and the scenery, with other issues periodically under discussion. Women are blessed with the ability to talk without a break for literally hours and inevitably miss many of the sights and sounds of a walk-in favour of covering as much verbal ground as possible. In fact, our family champions at this are Maureen and her Aunty Jean, who are so proficient in this skill that they can take a 'wee break' in the bushes without ever interrupting the flow of their conversation!

Talking of wee breaks, Julian stepped off the path to find a suitable spot behind a tree, only to find a CCTV camera pointing at him...in the middle of a wood!

We opted for the lower of two paths through a sparse wood that enabled a close view of Fernilee Reservoir. After a short, steep climb we emerged at the southern dam wall and a minor road that was our passage to the opposite bank. Across the way we spotted a clubhouse on the shores of the nearby Errwood Reservoir, with some sailing boat activity on the calm water, powered by a pleasant wind that was being squeezed up the valley. It looked a serene and tranquil place for a spot of lunch and, as we wandered along the road passing between the two reservoirs, we looked forward to a break and some coffee. "Errwood Sailing Club – new members welcome", said the sign at the end of the drive. There were several current members of the sailing fraternity busying themselves outside, seemingly clearing away after a morning's event that had evidently recently finished.

I approached one of them. "Do you mind if one of our group uses your toilet, please?", I said. Wendy was not accustomed to using what nature provides, unlike us hardened walkers.

"Sorry, no, they're private", she said. "If we let you use them, everyone will want to and they take a lot of maintaining", she continued. She had seemingly already dismissed us as four potential new members and had slotted us into the category of 'not our type'. I instantly withdrew any wayward thoughts of joining this closed shop!

"Well, thank you for nothing", I said gruffly. A nearby colleague of hers overheard the conversation. "There's some portaloos around the back, you can use one of those", he said. "We only have them as there's been an event today", he explained. I thanked him and decided to chance my arm at a second request.

"Is it okay if we take a seat on your bench while we eat our lunch?"

"We wouldn't normally allow it, but it's okay if you're not too long", he said.

"Thanks", I replied, through gritted teeth. I was fuming. I'm not sure what their sign means by new members being 'welcome', but if you're not allowed to use the toilet or sit down they'll do well to ever have any new members!

After what was probably the longest we've ever taken to eat our lunch, we removed ourselves from their precious bench and decided against a further toilet visit before continuing. We ambled slowly out of the gate and up the rising path in search of the Old Roman Road a few hundred metres up the hillside. The views along Goyt Valley opened as we gained height, rolling hills all round and both reservoirs now in view. The Old Roman Road was a rough track, classically long and straight, and in its day, was the primary route leading to Buxton. The final stretch of this had now become the A5004, which we followed down into town. Though not too long since our memorable lunch, we nevertheless treated Julian, Wendy and ourselves to tea and cakes at 'No.6 The Square'. It was a delightful way to end the day. After an hour or so we went off to find our B&B, Grosvenor House, while Julian and Wendy travelled back to Whaley Bridge to collect their car. By the time they returned to Buxton to drop off Maureen's rucksack it was raining heavily.

Just as we were musing over where to go for our evening meal that would avoid us getting too wet, my brother Bryan made contact. He later drove over from Nottingham to meet up with us. Great, we thought, we won't get wet. Wrong! He chose to park in a local pay and display expecting it to be near a pub, but we ended up trudging the streets in the pouring rain for 20 minutes trying to find one! Eventually we came across a local Mexican restaurant where we had a great catch up over dinner, once we'd dried off. He dropped us back at our digs, near enough to stay dry this time. All in all, it had been an enjoyable, restful day, which would set us up nicely for tomorrow's challenge!

We opened the curtains the next morning in hopeful anticipation, but we were instantly disappointed. It was still raining heavily. It always rains in Buxton. We shouldn't have been too surprised really, but perhaps the weather forecast not mentioning the 'R' word didn't help. After a perfect breakfast (one of the best of the whole walk), spent anxiously looking out across the Pavilion Gardens as the rain battered the roof of the Buxton Opera House, we togged up in our wet weather gear and stepped into the damp world outside. We had 17 miles ahead of us until we reached Congleton, some of which would be challenging even on a dry, clear day. We threaded our way through the puddled streets to reach the car park for Poole's Cavern, a vast underground limestone cave with amazing stalactites, from where our path would head up towards the folly that is Solomon's Temple.

A stiff uphill climb brought us out onto Axe Edge Moor, exposed, misty and sodden underfoot by the incessant rain. We gamely set out as planned to cross the moor for 2 miles and then drop down to the Dane Valley Way for low level walking, to follow the river of the same name. But we were soon unable to see any semblance of a footpath, the mist was rolling in, the rain was getting worse if anything and we were more than ankle deep in a quagmire of gorse and grassy hummocks.

"This is crazy", said Maureen, "can't we find a way round this? I really don't like the look of this mist, it's rapidly becoming thick fog".

"We can backtrack to the last lane and take that down to the A53, which is a very busy road though between Buxton and Leek".

"Let's get down there and take stock again once we're off this damn moor", she said, clearly not a happy bunny!" It was the sensible thing to do, even though I don't like going off a planned route, but safety must always be a priority. The two benefits on reaching a tarmac road are being back on firm ground and knowing that it's always going to lead somewhere, as roads inevitably do.

Just after reaching the A53 we spotted an oasis, a bus shelter and a brick-built one at that. "Let's get out of this rain for a few minutes and check the map again", I suggested. The bus shelter was very basic, but at least we could shake the rain off our clothes and decide where to go next. There was a turn about 2 miles down the road leading to the village of Flash, the highest village in England. We could connect with the Dane Valley Way a couple of miles beyond that and won't have gone too far out of our way.

"I'm cold, wet and fed up", said Maureen. Me too, I thought, but I wouldn't say so of course. Not because of any macho bravado, but I needed to get Maureen, and us, through this day and safely to Congleton, so keeping our spirits up was down to me.

"The next couple of miles will be unpleasant and watch out for lorries and water spray off their wheels", I said, "but after that we're on quiet country lanes for a while".

If there is such a thing as God, he'd clearly decided it was time to intervene, for as we left the shelter the rain eased right down, and the mist lifted. The A53 was busy and frequent use was made of the adjacent grass verge. Dangerous as it seemed, it was still preferable to potentially getting lost on the moors. Not that I ever admit to being 'lost' on a walk, again not through any vanity, I just prefer to say, "we're not lost, we just don't know where we are right now". If we're wandering aimlessly something usually comes along, maybe a lane or a farm building, that can be identified on the map and then, hey presto, we're no-longer 'lost'.

No chance now though of being confused. We were on the A53 and were regularly reminded of this by each passing vehicle. Relief is probably an understatement of how we felt when we finally reached the turn for the village.

"Well done, babe", I said, as we passed the sign duly proclaiming the village's fame as the highest in England. "And the good news is that we've just reached our 600 miles point...in a Flash!!" I said. I'm certain I saw a smile on Maureen's face as we marched on, still with 11 miles to go. In golfing parlance, we were now on the back nine. Yet being in Derbyshire, in middle England, it didn't particularly feel like we were, with Cheshire, Shropshire, The Cotswolds, the Lambourn Downs, the South Downs and 61 miles along the coast to Dover still to be completed over and 31 more days of walking.

It was still very cold, with us needing all five layers of clothing to keep warm. The days of tee shirts and shorts and 25-30-degree temperatures seemed a distant memory at that point. The scenery as we dropped downhill from Flash was impressive, though. Steep sided hills, green pastures, woods and a sweeping valley leading to the distant Rudyard Reservoir, all served to paint a classic countryside picture. I made a mental note to come back here one day, in better weather of course.

Once off the lane and on the Dane Valley Way, the going became very muddy underfoot following the recent onslaught of rain. Consequently, it was slow going through the fields and subsequent path as it zigzagged its way through the wood that follows the river on its weaving journey to Danebridge, some 4 miles further on. The village comprises of a single road with a few individually designed houses and nothing more, except for the small Wincle Brewery. It might be the right place for a pint, but it wasn't the right time for alcohol. We entered the brewery via two high sliding metal doors with no windows, but which were left open for daylight to enter. We found ourselves in the storeroom, piled high with barrels, a real-ale drinker's heaven on earth. Fortunately, they also offered coffees from a machine. With no traditional cafe-type facilities on hand, we were instead offered a metal beer barrel each to sit on. They were cold and uncomfortable, but we eagerly took up the offer just to get off our feet for a while.

At last the sun appeared and the skies were brightening up as we continued a riverside path along the Dane Valley Way, which 2 miles later would join up with both the Gritstone Trail and the Staffordshire Way. The going remained heavy on the grassy path, so after a review of the map we opted to use lanes for the final 4.5 miles and in so doing bypassed the intended climb to the 'Cloud' viewpoint.

As we reached the outskirts of Congleton, Maureen was clearly flagging, and to be honest I had very little energy too. It had been a long day and with the detour we'd taken to get off Axe Edge Moor we'd already covered our intended mileage. Our B&B was still 2 miles away though. My trusty map indicated a pub was just ahead of us, so I decided it was time to offer Maureen an olive branch.

"I think we should drop into this pub, grab something to drink and then call for a taxi to take us to our B&B", I said. "We've made it to Congleton, we've done our intended mileage by hook or by crook, and I think we both deserve to call it a day". Maureen didn't need persuading, so we headed down the incline and through the doors of the Coach & Horses. I ordered a couple of coffees and asked the owner, Mike, for the number of a local taxi firm for our ride into town.

"Walked far have you? he asked. "From Buxton today, but we started at the top of Scotland seven weeks ago and have been walking ever since", I replied.

"Wow, that's some walk. Where are you staying in Congleton?" he enquired.

"At the Queens Head", I said.

"Right, if you can hang on for 30 minutes I'll run you down there", Mike said. Another great and unexpected kind offer of support, which was thoroughly welcome. A few minutes later not only did he bring us our coffees, he brought over some hot cocktail sausages and a basket of chips. "Tuck in, on the house, and I'll give you a shout in 30 minutes", he said.

We were overwhelmed by such generosity and had soon recovered from our day, enjoying the hot coffees and nibbles. As he'd promised, 30 minutes later we were in Mike's car heading for town.

"Have you stayed at the Queen's Head before?" he asked.

"No, this is our first visit to Congleton", I replied.

"It's a bit of a football fans' pub. You realise England are playing Slovakia in the European Championship tonight don't you?" he said. "Could be a bit lively in there". At just £50 for a night's B&B I had been concerned how this place might work out, but it was directly on our route so I just had to book it.

Sure enough, as Mike turned his car into their car park, the Queens Head's patrons for the evening were gathering in the garden marquee, which was bedecked with England bunting. The outside of the pub also left no-one in any doubt how patriotic the owners were and where any local England supporters who might like a drink or two should be spending their next few hours! We said our thanks and goodbyes to Mike and made our way in. It was a bit of a challenge to get through the busy bar area with a couple of rucksacks to check in, but we managed it. We feared the worst, in that we felt more in need of a quiet night in than

143

anything else. Fortunately, our accommodation turned out to be in an adjoining annex and was as segregated from the England fans as any visiting supporters might be (not that we didn't want an England victory. In fact, if they lost it might turn out to be quite raucous later).

Once the dividing door was closed the annex was virtually sound proofed from the pub. The facilities were a marvellous surprise, three freshly decorated en-suite bedrooms plus a shared self-contained kitchen, with a fridge stocked with milk and butter, plus cereals and bread, and a long-distance walkers piece-de-resistance, a washing machine and separate spin drier – deep joy! We took full advantage of all that was on offer, having a late 'breakfast' to save eating out and putting a big clothes wash on. There was also very little commotion from within the pub, probably due to the match being a typical England bore-draw.

The next morning, we flicked on the TV just as the inquest into why England had failed to beat Slovakia was ending. These things don't last too long though, as we English tend to move on quickly from such non-events, particularly as there was a much more important matter to focus on. This was Tuesday 21st June, with just 2 days to go before the UK EU Referendum voting day. The BBC was now focused on that and the football result was already consigned to the record books.

To a large extent we'd parked any thoughts of the Referendum since posting our vote in Keswick. We'd done our bit and now it was for the remainder of the UK to decide. The pundits felt the result was too close to call, but we'd soon be finding out.

After making our final use of the cereals and bread provided in the kitchen we settled our bill, the best £50 we'd ever spent on a B&B. Once outside we walked through the beer garden from where steps led directly onto the path beside the Macclesfield Canal, which we followed for the first 3 miles of today's 16 miles stint to Church Minshull. A variety of canal boats were enhancing the scenery and it made for an easy, pleasant start to the walk. Leaving the canal to head west on the South Cheshire Way, we soon came to the delightful Little Moreton Hall, a Tudor house built between 1504 and 1508 in the classic black timber and white walls style that is frequently seen in the west of England. The wooden structure was very curved in places, and by rights it shouldn't still be standing, but it was a memorable site against the clear blue skies on another hot, sunny day.

The South Cheshire Way took us over several fields of easy walking until it reached the Trent & Mersey Canal just after the 7 miles point. We dipped under the M6 soon afterwards, signifying that we were well and truly in the west side of England and heading deeper into Cheshire. Just as we were contemplating taking a break, we came across an unusual sight, namely a golf course sign encouraging walkers to visit the clubhouse. "Welcome to Malkin's Bank Golf Club", it proclaimed, and it was open for lunch. A short path from the canal side took us straight there. Rolls, nibbles and drinks were ordered, for which we were charged club members' prices, with change out of £7. How refreshing and enjoyable it was to sit outside the club house, overlooking the 18th green. There was also a sign confirming that we were at the academy of Ian Woosnam, a great Welsh golfer of the early 1980's, during the heydays of Seve Ballesteros, Sandy Lyle, Nick Faldo and Bernhard Langer.

Suitably replenished we returned to the canal path and walked this for the next 4 miles. As nothing exciting was happening, Maureen donned her headphones and tuned into Radio 2. The surrounding countryside was then treated to her loud rendition of the classic Police song "Message in A Bottle"! After a brief stretch walking on lanes we joined a series of pastures for the final stretch. Surprisingly the going got quite frustrating, with waist-high grass to wade through, nettles galore saying hello to

145

our bare legs and umpteen step-up-and-over stiles to negotiate. On a hot, reasonably long day, this was getting very wearying and we were starting to look forward to our journey's end. The last mile to the village was on a minor road, which clearly served as the local race track, as the cars were speeding by us with little respect for two tired walkers.

With our B&B a mile or so on the other side of the village, we decided it would be best to eat before we checked in. We telephoned ahead to our next host, Ruth, who offered to collect us from the car park of the Badger Inn. "Our road is a bit dangerous for walkers, so it would be best if I collected you", she'd said, endorsing our recent experiences. The pub was the only place around for food, so we made our way in. It all looked very well furnished and carpeted and not really a place you'd think would welcome two hot, sweaty and probably smelly walkers.

"Can I help you?" asked the manager.

"We were hoping to dine", I said, "but we've just finished a long walk and are a bit worse for wear", I continued, trying to put it as nicely as possible.

"That's okay, no problem, come through", he said.

As we followed obediently through the pub I implored him, "please hide us in a dark corner somewhere, we don't want to impose on other people".

"Don't you worry about anything, you're more than welcome", he said. There was, fortunately, a corner table to be had, where we sheepishly unloaded our rucksacks well away from the other diners and eased into the chairs.

"It's no good", said Maureen, "the boots will have to come off, regardless of where we are". I followed suit. After that we parked any embarrassment and enjoyed a lovely dinner.

A couple of hours later Ruth met us outside the pub and chauffeured us to her delightful Primrose Cottage for the night. We slept soundly.

Every now and then a day on a walk of this length fits into the category "nothing much to write home about". Day 49 can be described that way, a 9-mile stroll across the Cheshire countryside to Tarporley. Ruth's husband Steven dropped us back at the Badger Inn from where we took quiet lanes to the nearby village of Wettenhall.

The first few pastures after that were plain and uninspiring, just grass, hedges and a few trees. These led to fields that were similarly ordinary, but were well populated with cows. So, we opted for the easy life, using the nearby parallel lane to walk to Eaton, our 7 miles point. We took a break there for coffees and snacks during which we were entertained by parents in a multitude of 4 x 4's trying desperately to park in what little space was available outside the village school, where sports day was underway. As we sat there enjoying the show Maureen's mobile pinged twice. Two more donations to our fund-raising efforts had been made, amounting to £50 and more importantly taking our total raised over the £2,000 mark. This was a great uplift, not only for the remainder of today's walk, but for the days and weeks to come.

After leaving the village, we turned off the lane to walk through Portal golf course and out the other side to reach Tarporley. Our trek predominantly westwards since Buxton would end here and we'd be heading due south again from tomorrow.

It was only 3.15pm as we checked in to the Foresters Arms, surprisingly well populated by drinkers for a Wednesday mid-afternoon. In some ways, it was frustrating to finish so early as we felt quite fresh and could have done more miles in the pleasant sunshine. However, when planning the route, the judgement was to either have a short 9-mile day or a long 23.5-mile day, as there was no accommodation to be found between Tarporley and tomorrow's destination of Malpas.

We awoke the next morning to greet a day that will always be significant in UK history. It was Thursday 23rd June 2016, UK EU Referendum Day, the day the nation would decide whether to remain in the European Union. Today would see the culmination of months of bitter campaigning by the Remain and Leave teams put to rest, while voters make their choice between the two simple options available. The polls would be open until 10pm, following which the TV channels would start their all-night vigils monitoring the results as they came in, each eager to be the first to announce the overall result. Which way will we go, we wondered?

Maureen and I could have the day oblivious to all of this of course, as we had already cast our vote and would now disappear into the countryside, giving it little thought again until tomorrow morning.

After a good breakfast, we set off on day 50, initially walking through a flowering potato crop, then further arable fields to join the Sandstone Trail. As we carefully made our way through the vegetables the impressive sight of Beeston Castle came into view, sitting atop the first real hill we'd seen in days, surrounded by trees. Our route took us past the main entrance to the castle at the foot of the hill and on towards the nearby Peckforton Castle, now a hotel.

We'd be on the Sandstone Trail for the next 10 miles. It was probably one of the best footpaths of the entire walk. The trail was great to walk on and excellently waymarked. A gradual ascent from the flatness of the Cheshire plains rose to a height of 200 metres by the 3 miles point, affording marvellous distant views towards Wales, on what was another gloriously sunny day. It was easy walking along the ridge of the Peckforton Hills and at 7 miles we reached the trig for the highest point of this trail at 268 metres. We descended to cross the A534 before rising on Bickerton Hill for the next couple of miles. We then returned to lower ground, passing the impressive Larkton Hall, before skirting round the gallops of the Manor House Stud Farm. We later learned that the stud farm is owned by former England footballer and legend Michael Owen (anyone who scores a hat trick against Germany in their own backyard as Michael did on 1st September 2001 deserves legend status).

We left the trail shortly afterwards and, after a few hundred yards on a lane, returned to a path between arable fields. The local farmers were harvesting grass for winter feed and it was fascinating to watch them as we walked. The main harvester was eating up the grass with its front rotors and spurting this out through a high funnel into the wagon of an adjacent tractor that was tracking its every move. No sooner was the wagon full and it was ready to take off to unload than another tractor and wagon swooped in to replace it, such that the flow from the funnel continued uninterrupted. The tractor drivers were so skilled at this that they could travel to the nearby farmyard, unload, then return to re-enter the field at the exact moment that the next changeover was required. It was pure clockwork. We could quite easily have watched this rural show until its final performance, which would no doubt be only once all the grass had been collected, probably finishing in the dark.

We walked the road for the last short stretch into Malpas. It was time for a break, so we stopped for coffee at The Old Fire Station, then picked up food at the local Co-op, before setting off for the last 1.5 miles of the day to reach our next B&B. I'd been looking forward to staying at The Hough, as on their website it looked like a very grand house. At the wrong side of £100 for the night it was also one of the top three most expensive places we'd be staying in, but B&B's in the Malpas area were very limited in number and this one was on our route.

As we turned into the driveway we gained our first sight of the house. It was indeed very grand, a country house of character, with a large oak front door and a classic bell-pull. We tried it a few times but gained no answer. I telephoned the owner's mobile to learn that she was on her way imminently from somewhere in the grounds. The door burst open and there was Emma to greet us. She was very animated, apologising for not answering the door sooner, but she was in the business offices, a converted building concealed behind a nearby tall hedge.

"Come in, come in", she beckoned. We stepped into the impressive hall, with doors leading off to rooms on all sides. "Let me take you up to your room, then join us in the kitchen for coffee", she said. The two-tiered stairs creaked as we headed up them, passing various paintings that adorned the walls. We were shown to a large double en-suite room, which overlooked the rear garden. This had a neatly laid patio, with roses and other colourful flowers in the adjacent borders, followed by a long-manicured lawn that led down to a swimming-pool sized oval pond. This was not an inappropriate way to describe the pond as we later found out that the family do swim in it regularly, albeit with schools of fish circling underneath them.

We re-joined Emma for a well-earned coffee and asked if it was okay to eat our food outside in the garden. "By all means, just make yourself at home", said Emma. I could live in a place like this, I thought to myself. As we sat around the garden table, watching the swallows skimming over the pond, with the majestic house behind us, it seemed a long way from what family and friends might think we "endure" on our long-distance walk. "This beats camping any day", I said to Maureen.

It had been a great day and the weather had again been perfect. As we relaxed later in our room, our thoughts returned to what was happening in the UK as voters completed their Referendum ballot papers. "I guess our hosts and most others around here in middle/upper class Cheshire are Remainers", I suggested to Maureen, who nodded in agreement. It would have been interesting watching developments on TV through the night, and had we not been on our walk we may well have stayed up until the early hours to watch the Referendum result unfold. But we needed our sleep in order to be fresh for tomorrow's walk to Wem. I couldn't help wondering though which way the vote would go, as I tried to drift off to sleep.

Chapter 9 – West Is Best

I awoke just after 5am and the first thing on my mind was the Referendum. Blurry eyed, I reached for my mobile and flicked it on. Its start-up jingle woke Maureen. "What's the result?" she asked: the Referendum evidently the first thing on her mind too – well, that and needing a wee! The headlines screamed the now immortal David Dimbleby short phrase "we're out". The UK had voted to leave the European Union. Brexit was for real! We dozed off for a while, but neither of us really slept again. By 7am we were up and getting ready. After watching the TV news, we made our way downstairs for breakfast, uncertain what the mood in the kitchen might be like.

"Morning all", bellowed Emma. "Hope you slept well. What did you think to the Referendum result?" And before we could utter a reply she continued, "We're leaving then. Quite right too. Everyone is these parts voted to leave. Farmers are fed up of the EU, as are businesses. We both voted to leave", she said. Then she slipped seamlessly into 'host mode' with "how many eggs do you want?" That was the last mention of the Referendum. We chatted about our walk and where to next. In no time breakfast was done and dusted and we were saying our goodbyes.

Ahead of us was a 13.5 mile walk to a place with the shortest name of the entire route: Wem. Its claim to fame is being the 'home of the Eckford sweet pea'; not very enticing and the weather was doing its bit to dampen proceedings too, necessitating waterproofs. After an initial mile of lane walking, we turned onto a footpath that would link us to the Shropshire Way in a couple of miles. Seemingly few people came this way, evidenced by very overgrown stiles, long grass and being strewn with various wild foliage, making it hard going.

Eventually, after much frustration, we came to cross the A525 just west of Whitchurch. It's also known as Wrexham Road, with the Welsh border a mere quarter of a mile to our right. We couldn't be any further in the west of England. An oasis in the form of the Alfresco Kitchen cafe was the other side of the road, so we felt duty bound to grab a quick coffee, if only to step out of the rain for a short while.

By 6.5 miles we were already disillusioned with the Shropshire Way. It was just a hard slog that we didn't need and when the sanctuary of a parallel lane became an option we decided to take it. Ordinarily we would always prefer to walk on footpaths, but on a walk where the aim each day is fundamentally to get from 'A' to 'B', a spot of lane walking rather than the challenge of an overgrown and poorly maintained footpath does not go amiss. In fact, we stayed on the lane, which was largely devoid of traffic, for the remaining miles until reaching Wem at around 4.15pm, by which time the rain had passed over. It had been one of those 'just do it' days and we were relieved to be walking up the short drive of our B&B, Aston Lodge.

We were met at the door by the owner, Gary, who marshalled us round the back of the building to what is described on their website as the Coach House, but we got the distinct impression that these annexed rooms were where muddy walkers are put. The room was okay though and after freshening up we took a stroll down to the local Fox Inn for some classic pub grub.

We were quite pleased to be heading out of Wem the next morning for no reason we could quite put our fingers on. Perhaps some places are just meant to be ones for passing through on a journey, never to be seen again. After a mile of walking through this unremarkable little town we re-joined the Shropshire Way at Oaklands, hoping for better experiences than yesterday. The weather was continuing to be overcast with the threat of rain. I think at this stage we were both needing a pick-me-up and fortunately we knew there'd be not one but two when we got to Shrewsbury after today's 15.5 miles. Maureen's Auntie Jean and Uncle Jack would be meeting us and spending the next two days walking with us. They are great characters, both in their late 70's, yet full of beans and living life to the full. We were looking forward to seeing them again.

Things started well enough, but at just under 2 miles we hit an early problem. We'd crossed a large grass field and were due to take a stile into the next one, a crop field, only to find it impassable. The crop in question was rape seed, which had turned from its vivid yellow flowers into the seed itself. Facing us was a solid web of interlocked plant stems, with sharp seed pods that can easily draw blood by scratching unsuspecting walkers. It was so dense that an army of Samurai warriors wouldn't have been able to hack their way through. Our only option was to divert to a nearby lane and follow this to reach the village of Clive. The village was an unplanned bonus and was lovely, with attractive cottages and an impressive church, alongside which a leafy path took us through to the adjacent village of Grinshill.

The Shropshire Way was much better underfoot and, apart from one climb over a fence where the route had been blocked off, it was pleasant, trouble-free walking. The route was okay generally for the next few miles, apart from another fence to climb over. By 8 miles we'd reached the main road into Shrewsbury, the A53 at Upper Astley, where we spied a pub with the unusual name of 'Dog in The Lane'. We decided to dip in for coffees, while sneakily eating the sandwiches we'd brought with us. The landlord is a talented artist who specialises in drawing caricatures of famous celebrities, the kind where their features are exaggerated, yet it's still crystal clear who each one is depicting. He's drawn hundreds of these and where does he choose to exhibit them...in both the ladies and gent's toilets!

The day was warming up nicely as we continued across a succession of pastures to Haughmond Hill, the highest point of the day, affording our first views of the now none-too-distant Shrewsbury. A muddy path through a large copse took us down to Uffington to find the River Severn. Here we turned right to head west, as the Shropshire Way tracked the river into town for the last 3 miles. The river does a large loop around the city rather than go straight through it, so we left the path as it neared the train station, a magnificent Victorian building, to cut across town. As we marched uphill towards our B&B we noticed a lady standing almost in the road, arms aloft waving in our direction. Although we couldn't make her out as such, it could only be Jean. At a safer spot to her left stood Jack and before many minutes had passed by us were united once more. We had plenty of catching up to do, which we did over dinner. It proved a challenge to get a table in the local pub as it was a busy Saturday night in Shrewsbury, not least because an annual food and drink festival was taking place, but we managed it and had a great evening.

Over the next 7 days we'd be walking through my favourite part of the west of England. We'd be heading due south from Shrewsbury, passing through Church Stretton, Ludlow, Tenbury Wells, Abberley and Great Malvern, before heading south-east via Tewkesbury towards the Cotswolds. We're familiar with some of these areas, especially Great Malvern where we were married, but some would be new experiences. When Jean and Jack plumped for the first two of these days I did make it known that they'd be long, hard walks and not at all flat. Jean will always say with total optimism "that's okay, we'll be alright". Jack is very hard of hearing and I'm sure that most times he doesn't know what Jean has let him in for, but he is very determined and always gets through whatever Jean has lined up for him.

Maureen's back had been troubling her again towards the end of yesterday, so I arranged for a local taxi to collect her rucksack, but this time it would be accompanied by one of Jean and Jack's. It made sense for them to take advantage of the baggage transfer too.

And so it was, after ensuring their car was safely parked for the 2 days they'd be walking with us, that we got underway for a 16.5 mile walk to Church Stretton. The walk profile was for 5 miles of gentle uphill, then 3 miles of flat, some challenging hills for the next 5 miles, before dropping down to our destination. Our pace would necessarily be slower than usual, and it would be a long day, no doubt. All the same, it was always a pleasure for 'M & M' to be walking with 'J & J'.

It was a sunny start to the day as we walked through the outskirts of town, passing the geo-garden and its controversial Quantum Leap sculpture, which is arch shaped and depicts the back bone and vertebrae of a dinosaur. It's ironically named, as the original cost of the sculpture was expected to be around £200,000, but due to problems with the supporting structure the final cost leapt to over £1 million!

After crossing the river, we picked up the Shropshire Way once again. It took 3 miles before we cleared the suburbs of Shrewsbury. The footpath then snaked through fields of waist high grasses before becoming a track leading up to the ridge of Lyth Hill Country Park. This summit affords great views across the valley below and across towards the distant mound of the Long Mynd. After soaking in the views for a short while from this lofted position, we followed the gravel path as it headed into the first valley and a series of pastures.

When Maureen and her Aunty Jean get together they talk constantly. In an obscure way, I marvel at how they keep it going and don't run out of things to discuss. It's like verbal chain mail. They seamlessly move on from one issue to the next. What's even more amazing is when they disappear behind the bushes for a call of nature, their talking doesn't even pause. They emerge from the greenery in the same conversation as when they went into it. Jack and I, on the other hand, chat a little and then have a few hundred yards of quiet, taking in the views, before we chat again or discuss the route.

At 9 miles, we took a lunch break, sat on the grass verge of a minor lane. It was a case of so far so good. Unfortunately, after lunch it all went horribly wrong. Within minutes of resuming rain had arrived, so it was on with the waterproofs. The rain soon became heavy, but the temperature remained mild. We passed through a gate into a long field to slog up a steep hill, with our heads down most of the time. About half way I looked up to see that the biggest bull ever was waiting for us at the top, in the one place we didn't need it to be, next to our exit gate. To our left was a barbed wire fence and a ditch, to our right the bull's lady friends were gathered some 200 yards away, but directly on line to a possible escape route. We stopped to consider turning around, but to our relief the bull must have got bored with our lack of progress towards him and decided to head back to his harem.

With the imagined mauling by the bull still fresh in our minds, we entered the next decidedly muddy field. The Shropshire Way markers that had largely been evident so far were suddenly none-existent. I wiped the rain from my map cover and tried to make sense of where we were, but what I was seeing on the map didn't seem to be what we were all looking at. After wandering aimlessly round the field trying to find the expected exit to the north, we all got a bit frustrated and decided we must find a lane somewhere and establish just where we were. We then heard an engine, and thankfully a farmer appeared at the field gate in his 4 x 4. On telling him of our predicament he steered us across a short field, to then pick up a lane to the village of Picklescott. That was just the ticket and once there we could review the route needed to get us to Church Stretton. It was still raining heavily when we arrived at the village and, fortunately, the village pub was open. No prizes for guessing that we went in, both for respite from the rain and to grab a few coffees. The Bottle and Glass Inn was like stepping into a different world to that outside. It was very warm in there, with a real fire burning merrily away in the hearth. Plenty of people were in, creating a constant buzz of conversation, and we were served with some of the best coffees we'd had on our journey so far. It was very cosy and quite frankly by the looks on everyone's faces we could have easily stayed there for the remainder of the day.

After about an hour I said, "I hate to say this, but we need to get going. The good news is that we won't now take the steep climb up the Betchcott Hills and onto the Long Mynd. The view today in this weather will be non-existent and we can take a lower-level route on a quiet lane to All Stretton, then on to Church Stretton."

"That sounds good to us", said Jean.

"There'll still be some uphill walking and it's about 4.5 miles to go yet, so a couple of hours walking to do", I said.

"It's still raining out there", Maureen said.

"We'll be alright", said Jack, "We've done most of it."

The uphill started immediately as we left the village, dipping slightly after a mile before rising again to a peak of 326 metres. The rain was in our faces and wasn't showing any signs of easing off. As we reached a crest, the surrounding hedges and trees ended, and we were on open moorland for the next mile. At least there was no chance of going wrong now and soon the final descent to All Stretton was completed.

The last 1.5 miles aside the main road into Church Stretton seemed like they were never going to end, but finally our B&B,

Victoria House, was reached. Access was via a single door off the main street into a short alley, where our host Diane, was there to greet us.

"Come on in, don't worry about being wet", she said.

"Are you sure, we're absolutely soaked", I said, compounded by there being four of us today rather than the customary two.

"Yes, no problem. Drop your boots onto these mats and let me have your wet gear, which I'll get dry for you, then I'll show you to your rooms", she said. Sensing a more-than-helpful host, Maureen asked if she could also do a clothes wash for us, which she readily agreed to. What a star.

We couldn't wait to get out of our wet gear and freshen up. After doing so Maureen dropped round to see Jean and check that they were okay.

"We're too knackered to go to dinner. Jack's already in bed asleep and I'll be joining him any minute", Jean said. Our eating place was only two doors away, but even for us that was far enough after an arduous day.

Unusually we both woke up that night at around 2am. We tend to sleep like logs after each day's walk and especially so after the longer ones. We soon realised why we were awake. From the adjacent room, we clearly heard Jack holler "Oh Jean...aah...aah".

"The old goat", I said to Maureen, "He's still got it in him, even after a long walk".

"As long as he's alright", Maureen said. A few more 'aahs' later and all was quiet again. We returned to our slumbers.

The next morning, we knocked on their room door just before 8am, then we all went down to breakfast together. As we sat around the table waiting for the coffee to arrive I had to beg the inevitable question.

"So, what we're you guys up to in the middle of the night then?" I asked.

"I had terrible cramp in both legs", said Jack, "and I had to shout to Jean to help me out of bed to stand up. Did we wake you up?"

"Well yes, but no problem, as long as you're alright now. I thought you were doing something much more enjoyable, you old devil", I said.

"I wish!" said Jean.

With breakfast over we gathered all our gear and started to settle our bill with Diane. "Going far today?" she enquired.

"Ludlow, 18 miles by our route", I said.

"That's a fair stint", she replied. "I was going to go to Hereford shopping today, but I can just as easily go to Ludlow and drop a rucksack off for you if you wish", she suggested. We readily accepted this great offer and just like yesterday Jean and Jack sent one of theirs too. This was really turning out to be our lucky day in this respect, as last evening Maureen had contact from a Gaynor Davies from the Country Walking Facebook Group, who said she'd meet us in Ludlow and take a rucksack on for us the next day. People are so kind.

I was a little apprehensive about today's walk after yesterday's experiences. After returning from the pub last evening I reviewed the route for today and decided to take out the first climb over Ragleth Hill. Whilst its one I've wanted to do for a while, I felt Jean and Jack didn't need to be doing it. The day would be long enough for them, and us, so I'd plotted a flatter first 3 miles through the valley via Little Stretton and Minton, to get us to

Mashbrook. This proved beneficial in getting their walking legs going again without a hill to climb.

From Mashbrook we entered a series of fields, detouring round a sizeable herd of Holsteins, before reaching the next village of Wistanstow. This had probably the most impressive village hall I've seen anywhere, a huge single storey building in the classic black and white design and easily the size of a small school. It was here that we passed through our 700 miles point, with 2/3rds of our journey now completed.

A stretch of quiet lane walking brought us to yet another village, Sibdon Carwood, where we re-joined the Shropshire Way. This had traversed the length of the Long Mynd before dropping down to meet us. It's a great walk up there, one that Maureen and I have covered several times. It would have been a long, steep haul to get up there from the B&B only to walk across it and then come back down again. Hence it didn't make sense to include it, but we'd be back again soon, no doubt!

At Sibdon Carwood we turned to head south-east and at 10 miles stopped for lunch in the grounds of Stokesay Castle. It's an unusual castle in that it's a fortified medieval manor house. Built at the end of the 13th century; it's in remarkable condition and is a mixture of dense castle walls with manor house architecture sitting on top of it. The gatehouse is in the style of the many black and white timber buildings in this area, except that in this case it was yellow! It was pleasantly warm as we sat there, and the signs were for a dry day.

The River Onny runs past the castle and this proved to be our companion for the next couple of miles until we crossed over it at Onibury Bridge, before heading due east to join the next one, the River Corve, which we followed as far as Ludlow Racecourse. The 'going' by now was 'tired-to very tired'. Jack was on autopilot, marching along with his walking sticks, but every now and then swaying to one side with weariness, a glazed look in his eyes. Jean, as ever, was getting it done, but the fact that she was quiet told me that tiredness was setting in with her too. Maureen was more than ready to reach the end and I knew that these last few furlongs would be the most difficult.

"A couple more miles and we're there", I said, aiming to motivate the troops. "Less than an hour's walking left to do. Keep it going." We left the Shropshire Way as we reached the main road into town and headed for our B&B. Jean and Jack had made it. I hope I can still walk 18-mile days when I'm pushing 80 years of age! There would be no difficulty in finding the B&B, as its name is its address, simply 130 Corve Street.

Soon we'd settled into our rooms, where our rucksacks were waiting for us, and had freshened up. It was time to meet Gaynor, who'd arrived to collect a rucksack. She'd come straight from her workplace and had gone out of her way to meet up with us, for which we were very grateful. We chatted briefly, handed over a rucksack, and then she was gone, home to her waiting husband and children just like any other day. As in similar exchanges, it felt all too brief to meet a 'virtual friend' for the first time and then part in the blink of an eye, not knowing if our paths would ever cross again.

The next morning, we said our goodbyes to Jean and Jack on the brow of Ludlow's high street. They headed off to the bus station to return to Shrewsbury to pick up their car, before travelling home to Derby. It wouldn't be the last we'd see of them on our walk though. They'd committed to meeting us when we reached Dover, which we were already looking forward to. All that remained before "we'll meet again" was another 340 miles and 24 days of walking.

We set off down the high street on our 9.5 miles walk to Tenbury Wells to reach the River Teme, which we'd be tracking all the way to our destination. After 1.5 miles of lane walking we came to the hamlet of Steventon, where we were due to transfer to a footpath, but the condition of it was an absolute quagmire. It was the type of surface that those who run extreme events might wade into and find themselves knee deep in mud. Not our cup of tea, so we continued along lanes to Ashford Carbonnel, a delightful village of individual houses, some with thatched roofs and often in the mandatory black and white design. Good paths ensued from there to our 6-mile point, Little Hereford Bridge, where the Tameside Inn stood invitingly on the riverside. It was a warm day and the walking had been thirsty work, so we felt justified on this shorter distance to drop in for some thirst quenching drinks and a snack.

As we returned outside we found it had clouded over and there was the threat of rain hanging in the distant sky. All had been going well so far, but how quickly things can change. On reaching Berrington Court my map indicated that the footpath went around the back of the local garden centre. Once in its grounds we got ourselves very confused, lost some time looking for the right route and to add insult to injury the rain started. It was then that Maureen reminded me that she had made a hair appointment for 2.30pm in Tenbury Wells.

"Where the hell are we?" she said, "We should never have come into this stupid garden centre. I'm going to be late for my appointment now". Most guys will know that this is a fate worse than death itself, to make the lady in their life late for her hair salon session! I responded with natural concern.

"Stuff the hair appointment, you can do that anytime, I don't need this hassle, especially in this weather", I said. The rain was bouncing off the ground by now.

"That's right, don't care...we're not missing my appointment", Maureen affirmed. "Get me out of here and let's march on".

I looped us back to the lane and did as she had demanded, walking at something close to twice our normal speed, in complete silence of course. There was less than 2 miles to go and I could see that, despite her anxieties, we'd make it to the salon with time to spare. The lane took us into the town and the holy grail was located just down the main street. It was 2.15pm when we landed.

"I'm not stopping, you can find me at the B&B when you've done", I huffed, and left Maureen to her unknown stylist. The Ship Inn was a few streets away, so after I'd checked in and calmed down, I decided it was best to return to the salon to collect Maureen, to ensure she didn't get lost. She was all smiles when I got there, the heat of the day had gone, and we were convivial with each other once again. We ate in at the pub that night, both of us in the mood for classic pub grub.

Some mornings you open the curtains, take one look outside and think 'why can't the weather forecast be wrong for once?' Or maybe it's something less polite and much shorter! The rain, as predicted by the Met Office, was bouncing off the nearby roofs and the pavement below. Today was not going to be very enjoyable, but it had to done. We donned our waterproofs before we stepped outside, geared up for the onslaught awaiting us.

It would be a good stretch today, 12.5 miles to the village of Abberley. We were now in Worcestershire and the original plan was to head south-east on footpaths for the first 6 miles before turning north-east for the remaining 6.5 miles, also on footpaths. This may sound peculiar, but two factors led to this scenario. Firstly, a lack of accommodation without going as far east as Worcester itself, which was too off route for where we were headed. Secondly, I'd planned this section using a book called 'The Great English Walk – a long distance walk from Chepstow to Berwick-upon-Tweed', whose route went this way to reach

Great Witley. This would have been ideal, except the only accommodation in Great Witley had closed since the book was written, so I revised the route by a few miles to nearby Abberley.

All that said, a day tromping across countless fields and pastures in pouring rain didn't give the route its original appeal and after yesterday I didn't want today to be any more arduous for Maureen than possible.

"I've changed the route for today, Maureen", I told her over breakfast, "so that the first 9 miles will now be on back lanes. This should make for good progress and be largely mud free. I think given the atrocious weather we just need to march the walk out and get there as soon as we can". Maureen readily agreed.

We'd now be trailing the River Teme due east, though we didn't see too much of it or much else for that matter due to the high hedgerows. The rain was incessant as we passed through several hamlets before coming to a confusing situation. The roadside sign stated we had reached Eastham and a little further along the road we came to Eastham village hall. Ordinarily this would all seem perfectly okay, except that my OS map showed this village to be ¾ mile to the north of us.

"This is weird", I said to Maureen. "We are definitely on the correct road, but I don't see how we can be in Eastham, judging by what the map is telling me".

"There's a guy just coming out of the village hall, let's check with him", said Maureen. The hall was decked with a large banner proclaiming "Save Eastham Village".

What he told us seemed obscure, but apparently where the village is shown on the map is near to what was Eastham Bridge, which spanned the river. Some years earlier the bridge had been brought down by floods and the government had so far refused to fund a replacement. The bridge would take cars onto the main road, for eastwards travel to Worcester or westwards to Ludlow, but since the bridge had gone the cars pass through the area we were now standing in. The locals in conjunction with the council had re-designated this area as the village and spruced up a building to become the village hall, to make a case for heavy traffic causing problems in the absence of the bridge. So far, the government was unconvinced, perhaps because, just as we'd experienced, not many cars came by this way!

At 9 miles, we reached the B4203, where we danced on and off the grass verge for half a mile during busy traffic, until we came to Stanford Bridge.

"We could do with getting out of this rain for a while", I said. "There should be a pub or cafe around here". And then like an island in the sea we spotted 'The Den', a rustic styled cafe, with a vintage boiler burning brightly inside giving a welcoming warm glow to wet walkers. Wooden bench chairs were available, which we felt less guilty about sitting on in our sodden gear. We enjoyed piping hot soup and coffees whilst we checked the final part of the route on the map.

"We've got 2.5 miles to go. We can either take the footpath route or risk another mile or so on the B4203, then a track to our B&B", I suggested to Maureen.

"It's a busy road, but I don't want to do any footpaths today, so let's risk it", she said.

Once back outdoors it was just the same, very wet and no prospect of it relenting. The experience was not at all pleasant, with lorries frequently spraying us and cars not always giving us much latitude, even though we stood off the road whenever we could. It was a relief to reach the track, which is the access drive to the private Abberley Hall School. It's an architecturally impressive looking school which was established in 1878 and

167

where parents today can deposit their child as a boarder for the princely sum of £7,500 per term! In the grounds is a distinctive clock tower, not unlike Big Ben, but around half its height.

We were now on the Worcestershire Way and stayed with it almost to Abberley. The sting in the tail was a final 1-in-3 uphill stretch, before dropping equally as steeply into the village itself. Our B&B, The Manor Arms, was the central point of the village surrounded by a few houses and nothing much else. The staff were very welcoming, despite our dishevelled and soaked state, and readily agreed to undertake a clothes wash for us. It was a very comfortable place, with great food served at dinner, which we felt was deserved after such a challenging day.

The next morning was brighter for several reasons. Firstly, the rain had passed through overnight and outside was looking decidedly like it was going to be a better day. Secondly and more importantly, our next virtual angel would be coming to meet us after breakfast. Kate Arthur from the Country Walking Facebook Group had been in touch with an offer of a rucksack transfer to today's destination of Great Malvern, a 17.5 miles hike for us, so a lighter load for me and none for Maureen would again be very welcome. We had good reason to look forward to being in Great Malvern once more, as it was there on the deliberately symmetrical time and date of 3.00pm on the 3rd day of the 3rd month of the year 2000 that Maureen and I were married. The significance of the focus on 'threes' was nothing more than a date that caught our eye and an available time slot at the registry office...and no, it wasn't the third time around for both of us, in case you were wondering (it was the second actually).

Just after 9.00am Kate appeared, and it was again lovely to meet the person behind an online name. We chatted for a few minutes and then, given we were a little off our route in Abberley and facing a long day, we hitched a short but important ride back up the steep 1-in-3 uphill lane to preserve our legs for a little longer. Kate dropped us at the driveway to Abberley Hall School where we re-joined the Worcestershire Way. The path travelled due south and soon the views opened, looking eastwards into the rolling hills of Worcestershire, while to the west the distant Black Mountains of Wales could be seen. The Worcestershire Way was well waymarked, with clear, well maintained footpaths making for effortless walking and good progress being made. Wild flowers adorned the route, especially vivid red poppies and purple foxgloves. Further along, close to a small brook, a succession of black dragonflies weaved past us.

The sun was also with us during most of the morning, but it began to cloud over as we reached 9.5 miles, where we came upon a typical country pub which beckoned us over to stop for a lunch break. We chatted with two other walkers as we tucked into freshly made ham sandwiches. It seemed for all intents and purposes like the scene from a Sunday stroll rather than day 57 of a long-distance walk. No doubt tougher times lay ahead, though.

Within 3 miles of resuming we entered the realms of the Malvern Hills, though the true Malvern's would be scaled and enjoyed tomorrow. For now, the path continued without problems until at 14 miles we parted company to join a bridle path heading east for a mile or so. This led onto lanes for the final descent into Malvern town. My original plan had been to stop over at the north end of the hills and then head straight up onto End Hill the next morning, but to my disappointment I couldn't get in anywhere. Instead I had to opt for a place in town.

The Pembridge B&B is tucked away on a quiet side road, just half a mile from the town centre. After freshening up we headed out, passing Montrose Hotel, where we stayed when we got married, before entering the central park where a Victorian building houses the Registry Office. Little did we know 17 years earlier that a future visit would be at the end of two months and 754 miles of walking from the top of the UK! What we could guarantee was that the night would not be celebrated as it was 17 years ago - we were very tired when we got back to the B&B!

We were up early the next morning for a quick getaway, as we'd another long day ahead of us. First into the breakfast room, we were soon greeted by our host Steve.

"I'll just have poached eggs on toast, please Steve", I said.

"Ok, you do the toast, I'll get the eggs", he said and turned to head in the direction of the kitchen.

I looked across the table to Maureen. "Did he just say what I thought he said?", I asked.

"Yes", she said, "Looks like you need to make the toast".

Unknown to Steve, making my own toast is one of my bugbears with B&B's. Even worse, I was now being asked to do it for part of my main meal. As a paying guest, I prefer toast to be brought to me. But it's also because toasters come in such an array of styles, that when making toast myself it either comes out anaemic or, having then sent it round again, burnt. I begrudgingly trudged over to the industrial size toaster residing on a table across the room. Adjacent to it pinned to the wall was a long description of how to use it – a red rag to a bull called Martin!

After reading the first few lines through my still half open, tired eyes I said "I can't be arsed with all of this. I'll just stick the bread in". I returned to our table to munch on my muesli, my back to the toaster.

A few minutes later Maureen announced, "there's smoke going up the wall. I think your toast is burning".

I went over, pressed the eject button and up popped two charcoal slices of what was once bread. That end of the room was filling with smoke and a distinct burning aroma. I pinched the edge of each slice and dropped it onto a plate. I then marched round to the kitchen and rang the bell to gain Steve's attention. He came to the door and looked down at the black slabs on my plate.

"You've burnt the toast. Didn't you follow the instructions?"

"I'm the guest here", I said angrily. "Just bring me poached eggs on toast, please". I turned and headed back into the breakfast room, without giving him the chance of a response. 5 minutes later the eggs on toast appeared, as originally requested. What a palaver just to get a simple breakfast. We quickly finished eating, grabbed our gear (just one rucksack – Kate Arthur had offered to do a second baggage run but couldn't collect it until later in the morning, so we didn't see her before leaving), paid our bill and set off in the direction of the town centre.

We love the Malvern Hills and have walked over them on many occasions. They are always a delight whatever the weather. Today looked good, not too many clouds around and every chance of us seeing the amazing views from the top. But first we had to get up there. We picked up a footpath opposite the magnificent Great Malvern Priory, passing through the well-maintained Rose Bank Gardens, with their impressive steel sculpture of two buzzards. It's not the longest climb up and is only a couple of hundred metres from ground level, but it's a 1-in-3 slope, so your legs still celebrate when the top is reached.

North Hill was first and, to save some energy for later, we took a level path past the Worcestershire Beacon rather than climb higher to the trig point, which we've enjoyed previously. The views were incredible. To the east the valley reaches out from the bottom of the hills right across to the M5 and beyond, as far as the eye can see. To the west lies Hereford and beyond this the Welsh mountains of the Brecon Beacons. As the Malvern Hills aren't one continuous range, it's necessary after each one to descend to a road, then climb back up the next hill. After dropping to Upper Wyche, we crossed the road to walk Pinnacle Hill before dropping again to Wynd's Point. Across this road sits the impressive British Camp, an iron-age hill fort, but before heading that way a stop at the excellent roadside cafe is a must. After a welcome coffee we resumed our journey, again taking a level path rather than heading up British Camp which also doubles as the Herefordshire Beacon. Instead we were steering towards a reservoir, from where our path descended to head east for the next few miles.

My intention was to join the Worcestershire Link footpath, clearly marked on my OS map. Unfortunately, I missed it! We couldn't find any way markers for it and noticed there were very few general footpath signs either. We tried in vain to enter one field indicated on the map, but it was a real battle against head-high overgrowth just to find the stile. Once through it there was no visible evidence that anyone had walked this way recently. Frustration was setting in, along with time being wasted for very little progress. I suggested to Maureen that we abandon any thoughts of the Worcestershire Link and take lane options for a while.

At just over 7 miles our lane reached a 'B' road that we needed to use for about half a mile. As we turned onto it we were confronted by a herd of long horned cows standing in the road. Either side were open pastures, without fences, so the cows had a free right to roam. The occasional car that came along eased slowly through them. Our choice was to either brave walking through them or take a significant detour. Our approach to cows is always to watch them for a couple of minutes to see if they are lively or not. These didn't seem to be, so we decided to go for it by walking along the white line in the middle of the road, since most of the herd were chomping on the grass verges either side of it, with just a few strays now on the actual tarmac. I took a walking stick from Maureen so that we had one each as we made our move. They gave us their haunting stare as they looked to identify who was invading their space. We know not to return their stare, which they deem as confrontational, but keep a sideways glance at them to know if they are in any way interested in us. Maureen was visibly shaking by now, whilst I nervously led us through, assuring her that we'd be okay. It was still a huge relief once we were clear of them and making our escape down the road.

In the absence of the Worcestershire Link there were virtually no other footpaths in this area. At 9 miles, we stopped for a short break while I reviewed the OS map. Instead of turning south-east to head for Tewkesbury I saw there was a way to continue eastwards for 3 miles to reach the River Severn, where a riverside path provided a route south. The river was reached an hour or so later where we joined the Severn Way. The grass was long, and the ground churned up in places, making it harder going than anticipated, but there was no chance of taking a wrong turn as we simply needed to follow the river for the remaining miles to our destination.

It was while attempting to take a photograph of the river that my mobile phone abruptly shut off, never to be revived. I later learned that the rain of previous days had managed to seep in through the outer shell and ruin its electrics. Maureen's mobile had survived okay, thankfully.

All was going well on the walk until the final long pasture before the path reached a major road, where we needed to access the bridge to get over to the other side of the river for our final stretch into town. We could see a large herd of cows in the distance, but felt relieved when they began to follow the farmer's tractor away from where we were heading. But then for whatever reason the tractor performed a180-degree turn and began heading straight for us. The cows dutifully followed and even injected some pace into their pursuit of the farmer. They were evidently a frisky bunch and we instantly looked around for alternatives to being in their company. Initially nothing seemed obvious to us.

"What are we going to do, I'm not going near them, they'll get us", Maureen said, anxiously.

"We're going to have to leg it over the barbed wire perimeter fence into the hay field over there and try to walk down the edge of it", I said.

Once at the fence between the pasture and the hay field, I held it down as best I could to enable Maureen to stretch over it. Once she was safely over I found where the fence was attached to a stanchion and gingerly climbed up it. As I straddled the fence I took great care to ensure my groin area cleared the barbed wire! It wasn't elegant, but I made it over okay. There was a very thin trough of earth along the field edge that we began walking along, still close to the fence. The cows were almost level with us now and several of them came to the fence, hung their heads over the top and belted out a loud and prolonged 'moo' to shake us up. We had to sidle 2 yards into the hay to avoid a close encounter and thankfully we all progressed in our opposite directions without further interaction. On reaching the end of the hay field and after looking back to ensure the herd was well away, we re-climbed the barbed wire fence to find our exit onto the bridge.

We followed the pedestrian path alongside the A38 into town and soon came across the impressive Tewkesbury Abbey. It's incredible to think that it was built in the early 12th century and survives intact to this day. It's been flooded a couple of times, most recently in 2007, but it looked in great shape, resplendent in the late afternoon sun.

Our B&B, the Abbey Hotel, is located almost opposite its namesake, and was originally two town houses that have been converted into one building. On arriving we learnt that Kate Arthur had yet to land with our other rucksack. She had been caught up in traffic, but this unfortunate reality of modern life (for those not on a long-distance walk!) ensured we'd see her again and could thank her in person for 2 days of excellent support.

We'd noticed as we approached the B&B that next door was an Italian restaurant called Salerno, an ideal place we thought for our evening meal. What we discovered later was that the restaurant is integral to the hotel, which was useful as when we went down to eat it was raining outside. How convenient to have an excellent Italian meal and then retire to our room without leaving the building.

A disappointment yesterday was that Maureen's daughter Jo couldn't meet up with us at the Abbey Hotel as planned, to then walk with us today to Winchcombe. Instead she would meet us there and walk with us the following day. Little did any of us foresee that this would turn out to be a blessing in disguise.

We eased our way out of Tewkesbury to cross the river and head east on the Gloucestershire Way. A mile or so later we crossed a bridge over the already hectic M5 motorway. After a short lane section through the village of Oxenton, which has more letters in its name than houses, we stepped into our first field of the day. It was probably one that had been left to fallow, as we had to wade through waist high wild grasses, then head-height reeds, some of which had been flattened creating a surface similar to walking on canes. It was tough going and the next field, although a different scenario, comprised of shoulder-high pea crops. It was like a jungle, hacking our way through using Maureen's walking sticks.

After a short break at the next village of Woolstone things really went wrong. We passed through a farmyard and our path should have been on our left. We simply couldn't find it and after going through three ploughed fields only to decide it wasn't right and turn around, we'd lost 40 minutes and ended up back in Woolstone.

By this time Maureen had totally had enough. She sat on a grass bank and said, "I'm not moving, I've had it with this path". I felt much the same, but a sit-in wouldn't get us to Winchcombe. It was also proving to be a very hot day and our water supplies were getting depleted. I reviewed the OS map and suggested we take a path to the nearby village of Gothering, then walk the final miles down a 'B' road. Gothering was quiet for a Saturday and, to our surprise and disappointment, its one shop had already closed for the day and it was barely 3pm. We headed down the road, which conversely was very busy with traffic. By now we'd more than covered our planned 10.5 miles of walking, but still had an additional 3 miles to do following our detour, in hot weather and with virtually no water left. I honestly couldn't see Maureen making it and I was feeling pretty fed up with how it was all going. So, it was time to be sensible and offer an olive branch.

"Have you got a signal on your mobile", I asked.

"Yes, why?" she snapped.

"I think we should phone for a taxi to get us into Winchcombe. We've done our walking and, let's face it, we've both had enough for today".

She didn't need more than the one olive branch! A quick Google search, followed by a phone call and a taxi was soon with us. Neither of us like resorting to transport and would only do so if we'd walked the equivalent of our planned route. But sometimes on a long-distance walk, when a day is just not working out and fatigue is also setting in, it's necessary to take the sensible option. We still had 19 days and 259 miles to walk and needed to be ready to go again in the morning.

After being dropped in Winchcombe we further recovered in a cafe, before picking up a few supplies at the local Spar shop. Unfortunately, the B&B I'd booked was 3 miles beyond Winchcombe, as all local accommodation had been block booked by a wedding party. Getting to it was not in the route plan though and a legitimate taxi ride soon got us there by early evening.

It had been an awful day. The Gloucestershire Way, like the Worcestershire Way link before it, was instantly forgettable. The two paths should have taken us pleasurably from the Malvern Hills, across a valley and on to Winchcombe, which they failed to do. However, I must accept some of the blame myself. That evening I went over the OS map to try to figure out what had gone so wrong. It was then I saw that my map was printed in 2001 and was therefore 15 years old. Evidently both the Worcestershire Link and Gloucestershire Way had been changed and re-routed since then. A harsh lesson learnt! Thank goodness that Jo hadn't been with us. I was confident that tomorrow's walk to Bourton-on-the-Water would be very much more straightforward.

Gordon and Yvonne, best B&B owners and accommodation.

Nearly at the border!

Maureen striding up Langstrath valley in the Lake District.

Sticking to coffee despite a break at the Winkle Brewery.

In Derbyshire with Wendy and Julian.

Jean and Jack joined us in the Shropshire hills.

Tom and Jo enjoying the Wardens Way, Cotswolds.

A deserved round of drinks with Gary and Angie.

Chapter 10 – Win To Win

Day 60 dawned on the next stage of our Caper. For the ensuing 7 days we'd be heading due south for 93 miles, taking us to Winchester.

How to bypass London and its surrounding areas to get to Dover was the dilemma when planning this section. I initially looked at this from a south-to-north perspective and found that a route keeping east out of Dover would need to reach the Greenwich Tunnel to pass under the River Thames, before heading into Essex and then north-east through Hertfordshire, Bedfordshire and Northamptonshire, which didn't overly inspire me. Going through the centre of London also didn't appeal, wonderful though our capital city is, as the aim of the walk was to be predominantly in the countryside. The third option I looked at was to pass up the west side of Greater London, which in turn meant going under London from Dover, taking in either the North or South Downs. This seemed a more rural option and would incorporate completing a National Trail. When I then considered how this looked coming down from the north, this third option linked best with our route down the west side of England. We would aim for Winchester and use the South Downs Way to Eastbourne, then walk up the coast to Dover.

Maureen and I stepped outside of our B&B just as her daughter Jo arrived with her husband Tim and their two children, Tom and Evie. It was great to see family members once again, with Jo and Tom joining us for today's 13.5 mile walk to Bourton-on-the-Water. Tim and Evie headed back home to Weston-Super-Mare, but would link up with us for dinner. This gave us another opportunity to dispose of Maureen's rucksack for the day, leaving it in Tim's car until we saw him later.

The Cotswolds Way provided an instant path from the B&B for the first 2 miles, rising a steep bank that afforded spectacular views back across the Cotswolds to the west. It was a gloriously sunny day, with a clear blue sky festooned with white bubble clouds. As the Cotswolds Way headed off south-west, we joined a lane that began quietly but for a few minutes was invaded by a motorcade of the MBG GT car club on a day's rally. Almost as quickly as the parade came by it was gone and the sounds of the birds signing was again all that broke the silence, apart from Maureen catching up in conversation with Jo of course. Tom and I paired up as we joined the Wardens Way, which turned out to be the best maintained footpath of the entire route. It was comprehensively waymarked throughout, and every field or pasture was perfectly maintained. The local farmers must be congratulated for fully supporting walkers' rights of way.

A series of classic Cotswolds villages would be visited on our route to Bourton-on-the-Water, the first of them being Guiting Power. On the village outskirts, we chanced upon some locals who advised us that a recent claim to fame for the village, which they also confirmed is pronounced 'Guyting Power', was the filming of singer Susan Boyle's Christmas video in the nearby woods. Apparently, it was undertaken the previous July and given a winter's makeover by spraying all the trees with artificial snow. This seemed strange to me, as Susan's homeland of Scotland has more than enough trees to serve this purpose and snow for that matter.

By now it was proving to be a very hot day, so an early stop on the village green was taken for a typical English picnic lunch, ably prepared by Jo and followed by a round of chilled drinks at the local pub. It was a fantastic family day. Maureen and Jo chattered happily while Tom and I discussed politics and the recent Referendum result. Tom is a politician in the making, with some very mature views for a 14-year-old.

The rolling Cotswolds countryside on such a perfect summer's day was a photographer's dream and we took many 'snaps' (not sure what the digital mobile phone equivalent word is) before stopping for further thirst quenchers in Naunton village.

There were several other walkers out today, as we ticked off the miles in the idyllic surroundings. The next villages encountered were the unfortunately named Upper Slaughter and Lower Slaughter. The name 'Slaughter' is derived from the old English word 'Slohtre' meaning a muddy place, which they may well be during damper times. Today they were picture perfect, strewn with cottages in Cotswolds stone, many with thatched roofs and an abundance of flowers lining the streets to add to their chocolate box image.

After a great day's walking, the crown jewel of the Cotswolds was reached, Bourton-on-the-Water. The shallow River Windrush is channelled down the main street, populated by numerous water birds, and crossed by low-level bridges every now and then. It's a tourist's delight and many come to visit, especially on such a classic English summer's day.

The Duke of Wellington pub, our accommodation for the night, was just along the main street. Tim and Evie were already waiting there to greet us and to hear about the walk. Soon we were joined by our close friends Angie and Gary, who had travelled down from our home town of Derby to stay over with us and who would be walking with us tomorrow. Suitably nourished, after we said our goodbyes to family members we spent some time catching up with Angie and Gary. To have such magnificent support from family and friends at this stage of our journey was very inspiring and much appreciated.

After a disturbed night's sleep, where we were woken on several occasions by unidentifiable 'noises' outside, we set off with Angie and Gary on our 9.5 mile walk to Burford. On paper, this walk looked to be very ordinary and I always worry when friends have travelled some distance to be with us that the walk turns out to be a disappointing one. However, it was more of an opportunity to be with them again, not having seen them since April. We eased out of the village, passing a few fish farms, to follow a lane to Great Rissington. From there a good path took us through a succession of fields, making for easy walking. As we came to the 5 miles point we celebrated reaching 800 miles overall on our journey. The path joined a lane to Great Barrington, passing the delightful Barrington Mill, before crossing the river into Little Barrington. Size seems very important in these parts! With 7 miles now completed all that remained were a couple of miles or so on a quiet back lane taking us into Burford, a town bigger than the two 'greats' plus the 'little' added together. It had been a very pleasant, easy meander, but we still felt that traditional tea and scones were merited on arrival, which were taken in the garden of a local pub.

That evening I checked the condition of my walking boots, mindful that 800 miles is generally what I'd expect to get out of a pair before they show signs of wear and tear. Sure enough, the left boot had cracked where it bends with the toes and I had doubts that it would last the journey. I decided to telephone Cotswolds Outdoors in Nottingham, just as Maureen had done previously from Scotland, to order a new pair. I asked for them to be sent to the home of our neighbours in Derby, Denise and Brian, as fortunately they would be meeting up with us in a few days' time and would be happy to bring them down to us. As ever, Alan Walker and his team in Nottingham came up trumps for me and mailed the boots out the same day.

While I was making my call, Maureen checked how the sponsorship was going.

"Brilliant news, we've now more than doubled our target and have reached almost £2,500. People are so generous", she said.

The next morning Angie and Gary walked a little way to the edge of town with us, passing the rows of traditional terraced Cotswolds houses, before we said our goodbyes. As from today we were embarking on new walking territories. We were now in Oxfordshire, an area we'd never walked in previously, and the remainder of our journey would take us through the yet unexplored Home Counties of Berkshire, Buckinghamshire, Essex, Sussex and Kent. From our base in Derby we tend to either walk locally, head west or go north to such as Yorkshire, the Lake District and beyond. It seldom occurs to us to go due south or south-east, the nearest being heading south-west into Somerset, Devon and Cornwall. Part of my planning process was therefore to seize the opportunity of walking through these new-to-us areas of England.

Today we were back in our familiar situation of just the two of us heading off together to our next destination, this time Faringdon, a solid day's walking of 15.5 miles in front of us. We soon picked up our footpath, which sidled down the edge of several fields before reaching a footbridge over a beck, with nothing obvious to suggest why that spot holds the grand title of Mount Zion Bottom. There was no resemblance to Jerusalem or Israel as far as I could discern. The path was very clear and easy to follow, soon coming to the village of Shilton where we took a rucksack break, which we repeated 3 miles later at Alvescot.

The day was really hotting up as we crossed a road to the riverside Swan Hotel at 9 miles, an ideal place for drinks and to eat our sandwiches under the shade of a sun umbrella. Several boats were moored on the river, which in fact was the Thames, alongside which we spotted a sign for the Thames Path National Trail on the opposite grassy bank. It's a walk we'll no doubt undertake one day, from its source at Thames Head, a few miles south-west of Cirencester, heading south-east to reach and pass through London, before ending at the Thames Barrier.

We contemplated that we still had 6.5 miles to do in what was by now a scorching day.

"It's very hot, isn't it?" I said to Maureen.

"Yeah, I'll be happy to be finished today", she replied. Maureen finds it hard going once temperatures reach 25 degrees or more.

"Well, looking at the map, our footpath heads south-west for 3.5 miles before turning due east for 3 miles to Faringdon. There is a more direct route down the road we've just crossed, which is only 2.5 miles. Whilst we've been sitting here I've noticed that very few cars are going up or down the road. We could take a chance that it remains quiet, if you'd sooner take the shorter option?" I said.

"Sounds good to me", said Maureen.

Thankfully the road did stay quiet, with only the occasional vehicle causing us to dip onto the grass verge and within the hour we had reached Faringdon. Our B&B was the very ancient looking Old Crown Coach Inn, built in 1664, with plenty of dark wooden beams outside and inside. It had proud new owners who gave us a brief tour on route to our room. It felt steeped in atmosphere as we were led across the cobbled courtyard to climb the external Elizabethan stairway, which originally led to an upstairs courtroom, via many a creaking floorboard and a nearby room that is reputed to be haunted. Let's hope whoever it is stays in their room tonight.

That evening we received a text from our friend Pam, whom we'd met for the first time in 2015 when we were all on a guided walk around the Mont Blanc massif. It was a 13-day high level trek starting in Chamonix in France, passing into Switzerland, then into Italy, before returning to France to complete the clockwise circuit of this amazing part of the Alps. Pam confirmed that she would be able to meet us in the morning and walk the 12.5 miles to Lambourn with us. We replied by inviting her to take breakfast with us at the Inn.

At 8am Pam arrived, having travelled from her home in Wotton Bassett. It was great to see her again and we had a good catch up over scrambled eggs on toast! Pam is a very vibrant individual, always on the go and forever seeking new adventures. She's travelled far and wide across the world and always has a shopping list of places she's about to visit, walk across or climb up!

The first mile was spent alongside Faringdon's busy main road, before we picked up our first footpath. It was very overgrown and proved a bit of a battle to get to the village of Little Coxwell. From here the path improved and took us through crop fields to Longcot, where we had our first stop of the day. The weather was being kind to us as we continued through further arable fields, where the huge blue sky seemed to fall all the way to the ground. An old tunnel took us under rail lines to reach a lane. It was just an ordinary back lane but one that will live in our memories for a long time as a place where we unknowingly made a poor decision.

Rather than take the easy, tempting option of walking on the lane, we agreed to stick to the planned route that would make use of what the OS map showed as 'Hardwell Lane (track)'. It looked ideal on the map and was a more direct route than the lane to where we were heading. As we ventured down it the first 100 metres or so were quite overgrown, but we thought it would probably improve before going much further. We were so wrong and soon found ourselves even more immersed in greenery, battling with head-height plants and nettles, several taking advantage of Maureen and myself wearing shorts to sting us repeatedly. Pam, through experiences similar to this, never wears shorts. I can easily say it was as overgrown as any path I've ever walked on. In desperation, I hacked a way through to an adjacent field and after straddling a hedge we finally escaped our torment. We paused to treat the nettle stings, then ambled across the field to a stile which took us to, you've guessed it, our original lane, a mile further on from where we'd left it.

A steep walk up the lane led us to a picnic area on White Horse Hill, where we stopped for lunch and to recover from our ordeal. The views back across the miles to Faringdon looked impressive, peaceful and uncomplicated compared to the trials and tribulations we'd just encountered. Once refreshed we headed out on the hillside to the Uffington White Horse, a spidery like creature formed from deep trenches filled with crushed white chalk and almost unrecognisable as a horse. More interesting were the nearby mounds where once stood the large Iron Age hill fort of Uffington Castle, traditionally sited on the highest point of the hill and affording 360-degree views back to Oxfordshire and ahead to Berkshire. The traditional 'look at us we've reached the trig point' photos were taken before moving on.

Once over the top of the hill we turned west onto The Ridgeway National Trail and completed no more than 75 metres before leaving it again, to head south on the Lambourn Valley Way. We'd be following this for the remainder of the day and throughout tomorrow. We were now on the famous Lambourn Downs, a vast open space populated with numerous gallops for the multitude of racehorses that are trained here. We soon came along two discarded horse shoes which we picked up for souvenirs. It was easy walking now, with no difficulty in following the route through to Lambourn itself. We dropped into

The George pub on the high street for a well-earned cold drink and were not surprised that horse racing was showing on the television. Lambourn is a very horsey place.

Thirsts quenched we took the short walk to our B&B, Dormer House, on the edge of town. Pam had driven to Lambourn earlier in the day and left her car there, before taking the bus to Faringdon to meet us. On reaching our B&B Pam took a rucksack from us to leave in her car, which tomorrow she would park at our next B&B in Newbury, before repeating her process of today by taking a bus back to Lambourn to once more join us for breakfast. What fantastic support yet again.

Pam arrived bright and early the next morning and enjoyed breakfast with us, dished up by our excellent hosts Wilf and Carolyn. It had been a great stay overlooking the Berkshire Downs and it would have been easy to take an age with breakfast and ease into the walk mid-morning. But day 64 and a 12.5-mile walk beckoned. I donned my rucksack and the three of us headed off back through town briefly to re-join the Lambourn Valley Way.

More villages would be passed through today and it wasn't long before we reached the first of these, Eastbury. The path then meandered through hay fields until reaching the picture book village of East Garston. Wood framed houses with thatched roofs lined the quiet main street, alongside which the babbling River Lambourn slid by. The path continued to wander through golden fields on hay, which rose away from us up gentle slopes until they met the clear blue on the horizon. It was another perfect summer's day.

At Great Shefford the sound of birds above us gained our attention. There were two Red Kites circling above, but amazingly they were soon joined by a further six, providing an aerial display to behold.

"Red kites were re-introduced into this area to boost numbers", Pam advised us. Evidently it had been successful.

The next village of Weston soon appeared, where the peace and tranquillity became infected with the progressively louder hum of traffic from the nearby M4 motorway. A mile beyond Weston the path made a short but steep ascent to a footbridge over the intruder, which I decided to give the briefest of glances to, preferring to move beyond it and back into our rural landscape.

We clocked up 9 miles just as we entered Boxford, where a roadside sign for its local pub enticed us into stopping for cool drinks and to eat our sandwiches. On resuming our enjoyable trek through the Downs, two more miles were completed before reaching the grounds of the Watermill Theatre on the outskirts of Bagnor. It was a pleasant place next to the river and we decided to take a quick break on a bench in the grounds before the final push for Newbury. Evidently there was an afternoon performance in progress, probably for visiting school children, for every 30 seconds or so we observed a theatrically dressed individual appear from a door at one end of the building, run along the outside and dive through a door at the other end. It was surreal and seemed as if we were sitting back stage rather than in the garden.

Unfortunately, we couldn't stop for more entertainment on this occasion and set off for our final couple of miles. After crossing a bridge over the busy A34 our route took us through a golf course at Donnington. There were paths everywhere, ostensibly for the golfers, but no way markers that we saw, so we made a judgement call on which path we needed and followed it until we reached a set of exit gates. Once on the pavement outside the course we figured we were not where we thought we'd be, which was confirmed by a local chap whose gardening exploits were briefly interrupted by three disorientated walkers.

Once back on course, as it were, we marched along the main road leading to Newbury town centre to reach our B&B for the night, the appropriately named Pilgrims Guest House. Pam's car was resident in their car park.

"I can hang on to Maureen's rucksack again and take it now to your next B&B, if you wish", offered Pam. We couldn't possibly decline and after sorting out a few things we needed for the next day, we repacked it and handed it back over to Pam. It had been great walking with her and we were very grateful for how she'd put herself out with cars and buses and taking a rucksack on for us. Wonderful help and support like Pam's and many others were crucial in helping us to achieve our goal. We said our goodbyes and hoped it wouldn't be too long before we were in her company again.

I awoke the next morning instantly looking forward to the day. We'd got 16 miles ahead of us, though it wasn't so much the walk that I was anticipating but two places along the way. They were historically very, very different, both having rural inferences in their names. I hoped that Greenham Common and Watership Down would be as interesting to pass through as I was imagining.

We set off to walk through Newbury town centre to reach the River Kennet. It was the last day of the working week and Newbury was already bustling with people dashing to their offices, branded coffees in hand, and traffic queuing up to get to who-knows-where in a hurry. Dodging pedestrians down the high street brought us riverside, where we turned east before locating a footbridge, crossing the river and heading south again. We snaked through a few more streets, already eager to end our brief reunion with everyday life and go back to our 'bubble' in the countryside once again.

Newbury Racecourse was the first place of note, confirming we were on the right track! It was relatively quiet, being a nonrace day, as we ventured ahead on back lanes aiming for the suburb of Greenham. Back in 1981 Greenham Common became international news when a Women's Peace Camp was established to protest against nuclear weapons being sited at the Royal Air Force base. In September of that year 36 women chained themselves to the base's fence in protest at the British government's decision to allow cruise missiles to be located there. I remember seeing the almost nightly images of the protesting women on the news channels as their numbers swelled. They orchestrated their first mass blockade of the base in May 1982, with 250 women protesting. The camp was active for an incredible 19 years before being disbanded in the year 2000. I was keen to see what evidence remained of the camp or what tribute, if that is the correct word, had in some way been created there to record the women's valiant efforts. As we walked through the western fringes of the common, now heavily populated with trees and shrubs rather than the open common I was expecting, the answer soon became clear...nothing!

Apparently, the camp was inaugurated as a Commemorative and Historic Site on 5 October 2002, when seven standing stones encircled a 'Flame' sculpture representing a camp fire, but it was demolished in September 2013 after being vandalised many times. We both felt, whatever views we may have on this issue, that it was a shame there was no longer any indication here of such a significant occurrence in English history.

After leaving the common and crossing a main road we took a footpath that soon became another 'Hardwell Lane' experience, horrendously overgrown with shoulder high nettles that we battled through to reach another road only 100 metres away. Thankfully this turned out to be the quiet back road I was hoping for, but I had the distinct feeling that the day wasn't really going that well.

"Are you okay, Maureen?" I tentatively enquired.

"I suppose so", she said. "It's not exactly the most stimulating day, is it?" she said.

I couldn't help but feel, as the person who convinced Maureen to take this walk, that every day should go well and be enjoyable. When I know it isn't, it worries me, especially on long days. At least it was straightforward walking now, with footpaths taking us to Sydmanton, where we stopped to eat our packed lunch. We were just over half way, the weather was decent and a mile or so down the road was our next place of interest, Watership Down.

Just the thought of Watership Down instantly starts me humming the immortal 'Bright Eyes' song performed by Art Garfunkel in 1979, though actually written by Mike Batt who had earlier found fame as a Womble (younger readers will need to make use of Google at this point). The book was written in 1972 by Richard Adams with the story surrounding a small group of rabbits who needed to leave their warren to establish a new home, which they ultimately did at Watership Down. It became an animated film in 1978, which I remember seeing parents taking their little ones to see, only for them to leave the cinema in tears as it wasn't the pleasant film about fluffy rabbits that they were expecting!

As we walked up the quiet lane on the west side of Watership Down, we were afforded clear views across the expanse of grass that stretches across hillside, curling round to the famous warren where 'Fiver', 'Hazel', 'Blackberry' and many others (they are rabbits after all) made their new home. We gazed across expectantly and what did we see...nothing! There wasn't a single rabbit to be seen. We wondered if we were in fact looking at the wrong hill, but a check on my OS map confirmed it was the real thing. After a moment of disappointment, we continued ahead, opting to stay on the lane as it was virtually traffic free, while the intended footpath took a decent detour to the east. The surrounding countryside was impressive, with rolling hills of hay interspersed with plantations of trees. We passed through Hare Warren Farm and soon afterwards came to Hare Copse and what did we see...something, at last! Several hares were sitting upright on their haunches looking across at us, before resorting to all fours and tearing off into the distance in a matter of seconds. More lanes took us the final miles to our B&B named, as you've probably guessed, The Watership Down Inn. As we checked in we mentioned our dismay at not seeing any rabbits on the Down.

"Following the success of the book and film in the 1970's the rabbits were left unchecked and reached epidemic numbers. They were ruining crops and became pests really, despite the tourist interest. The decision was taken to cull them, but unfortunately they did too good a job and wiped them out completely", we were told by the receptionist.

When we reached our room, we found a copy of *Watership Down*, signed by the author, who we later learned had stayed there on several occasions.

I awoke the next morning all bright eyed and bushy tailed, ready to tackle the day's 14 mile walk to Winchester, a place I'd been really looking forward to seeing. Maureen, though, was suffering with her back and I knew I'd have to nurse her along to get her there, probably with a stint carrying both rucksacks at some point. I also knew there'd be little on route to distract her, as when planning this stretch it seemed like a 'just do it' day. But Maureen's determination knows no bounds and after taking a couple of painkillers it was boots on as usual for the 66th consecutive day.

Lanes and tracks took us the first couple of miles before we crossed the busy A34 to locate more of the same. A succession of these would run generally parallel to the A34 most of the way, though far enough away not to hear the traffic. Nothing of much interest to see, as expected, but at least the good weather was continuing with no rain now for the last 10 days.

The approach to Winchester was a strange and unexpectedly noisy affair, however. We'd left a lane to join a footpath crossing two large fields before reaching the outskirts of town. The tranquillity was ended by the sound of scrambler bikes coming from a nearby motocross circuit. On leaving the last of the fields there was a warning sign for those heading the opposite way. It read, "Danger – Unexploded ordnance within this field - it may explode and KILL you". It was a pity there wasn't a similar sign at the other end where we entered!

The path veered over towards the A34 and although we were separated from seeing it by high and dense trees, the traffic noise was absolutely deafening. Just as it was becoming unbearable the road turned east, with our path passing under it as we headed off in our separate directions. No sooner had the traffic decibels rescinded than the next unexpected noise greeted us...gunfire. It was impossible to discern where it was coming from and who was causing it. Unfortunately, in the uncertain world we live in we immediately thought the worst and that someone may be firing indiscriminately at anyone or anything that moved. We carried on nervously until we reached a main road, where people were queuing at a bus stop as if nothing was happening.

"Excuse me, do you know what the cause of all the gun fire is?" I asked a chap at the end of the queue.

"There's an ATR up the road, mate", he said, expecting that would mean something to me and allay our fears.

"What's an ATR?" I asked.

"An Armed Forces Training Range", he said, "A firing range. They're practicing".

"Oh, cheers mate", I said, slightly sheepishly. I think we'd probably been out in the sticks a little too long, but it was an anxious few minutes.

Maureen's painkillers had done the trick in almost getting her to our destination and it was only as we entered the outskirts of Winchester that I took over her rucksack for a while. As we passed through the pedestrianised streets we picked up some lunch and then ate it as we sat outside the hugely impressive Winchester Cathedral in the afternoon sun. It is an immense structure, one of the largest cathedrals in Europe and has been on its current site since the year 1093. The original cathedral was built on a nearby site in 642, but was demolished when the present one was completed. To contemplate the history that has occurred in this area, the UK and the world at large since the cathedral was opened over 900 years ago is just mind blowing.

"Let's find our B&B", I said to Maureen. "I'm looking forward to this".

Wolvesey View B&B was a short walk to the rear of the cathedral and is so named because it looks out on the ruins of Wolvesey Castle, which was where the town's bishops once lived. It was not so much the B&B as the owner I was intrigued to meet. He looked from the website like a retired university professor and he sounded like one too when I called him to make the booking. John greeted us warmly and invited us in to the detached house nestled down a secluded cul-de-sac. We immediately sensed that it was his home and that he rented out a room, rather than purposefully being a B&B. He led us to the room and showed us the bathroom on route, which he also used, and there was no en-suite. To say it was a throwback to the 1970's would have been generous. It clearly hadn't been updated for decades. In saying that, our room was full of character and wouldn't have been out of place in Glastonbury, with a patchwork bed cover that was probably handmade and books everywhere. It is no exaggeration though that we could write our name in the dust on the top of the bookcases, because we did it! The room hadn't seen a duster or polish for a long while. We pulled the bedclothes back and the bed was clean enough, so despite everything we opted to stay, as we probably had little chance of finding anywhere else available on a Saturday night in July.

Our great neighbours, Denise and Brian, had travelled down to meet up with us and arrived at the B&B just before 7pm. We decided on pizzas for dinner and found a local pizzeria a few minutes' walk away. They had been watching over our home throughout our 11 weeks away, ensuring the mail didn't pile up, posting our prepared packages on designated days with our next batch of maps, checking that the gardener I'd hired to cut the grass every two weeks turned up and were even starting our car up once a week, taking it up and down the driveway to stop the brakes from seizing. They are just the best neighbours anyone could want.

"We've got your new boots in the car", Brian said.

"Great, thank you for bringing them down. I hope you won't be angry, but I've decided to risk it with my current ones. I sounded out people's views on the Country Walking Facebook Site that we follow, and most people said I'd be better to finish the walk in worn-in boots than use new ones, providing they weren't letting in water, which they aren't".

"No problem", said Brian, "Whatever you feel is best".

After a wonderful meal, we returned to our B&B, hoping we'd get a good night's sleep and not wake up covered in bites! We said our goodbyes to Denise and Brian, who were off holidaying in the area for a few days.

We made it through the night okay and, after briefly freshening up in the none-too-clean bathroom, we went down for breakfast. The first thing we noticed was a cat roaming around the kitchen's work surfaces. John was stood by the cooker, on which several saucepans that looked like relics of the last war were ready to do our bidding.

"Morning", said John, "What can I get you for breakfast?"

"We'll just have cereals, thanks, as we ate a big meal last night", I replied. This was mostly true, but we also didn't want to risk having anything that came out of the kitchen or that didn't come out of a packet. We finished in record time and then made our escape. John was a nice guy, a bit of a character. He turned out to be a local authority worker in his working life, rather than the academic I'd fancifully imagined he was.

Our journey from Winchcombe to Winchester had been a great experience. We still had 160 miles to go until Dover, but out of a walk of 1,041 miles, we were arguably about to enter the home straight, though with plenty of England still to see and enjoy. It seemed a long, long while since Cape Wrath, where we looked out onto the Atlantic Ocean and yet tomorrow, amazingly, we would gain our first sighting of the English Channel.

Chapter 11 – It's Downs Hills All The Way

Being greeted by light rain as the door to the B&B closed behind us did not dampen our enthusiasm and sense of excitement for today's walk, day one of the South Downs Way National Trail. We had been looking forward to this for a long while. It would take us the next 8 days to complete the 105 miles to Eastbourne. For now, we had 12.5 miles to go to reach Exton. For the first 2 days of the trail Maureen and I would be enjoying each other's company, alone together as it were, walking hand-in-hand, as often as the route or the temperature allows us to. But for the remainder of the route we would be joined by two more friends from the Mont Blanc tour, Chris and Jane.

The official starting point of the South Downs Way (SDW) is the statue of King Alfred the Great, the former king of Wessex, who died in Winchester in 899AD. It's located in the high street, a few minutes' walk from the B&B. With wet weather gear donned, we set off and soon found 'Alf' standing proudly on his plinth on a grass refuge between two lanes of traffic, holding his sword aloft in triumph at having defeated the invading Vikings. From there a short spell of lane walking took us out of the town, to cross a bridge over the M3 leading to a footpath through fields. The wet and humid weather was causing significant mist, with visibility initially down to 50 metres. A lone walker suddenly appeared out of the gloom, heading towards us. We stopped for a brief chat and learned that he had completed the SDW in an amazing 3 days and had camped overnight too. Within half an hour or so the rain had stopped and the mist lifted, enabling us to see and enjoy the rolling countryside that is typical of these Downs.

As a National Trail, the acorn symbol accompanied the yellow way markers on all trail posts, making route finding easy. The path surface enables the trail to be used by runners, horse riders and cyclists, and it wasn't too long before we'd crossed paths with participants in each of these enjoying their Sunday morning exercise. The route was undulating but nothing too arduous, and with the weather improving all the time it made for enjoyable walking. At 10 miles we reached Beacon Hill, which being perched up at 201 metres afforded great views all around. The most exciting of these was the one we'd anticipated, our first sight of the sea. It may have been some 20 miles due south at this point, but it signified for the first time that we'd traversed from the top of the UK to the bottom. We gave each other a celebratory hug before continuing the walk for the final 4 miles, along the Meon Valley. There was an anxious moment when Maureen spotted what looked like a herd of black cows gathered on the path approximately half a mile ahead of us. Our suspicions were raised though, when they didn't seem to be moving much, if at all. As we progressed towards them it dawned on us that it was in fact a field of hay that had been harvested into bundles, wrapped in black plastic and left in the field!

Accommodation on the SDW is either scarce, expensive or both. Consequently, this stretch of our walk and through to Dover proved one of the most problematic for making B&B bookings. Exton didn't offer anything realistic for walkers seeking a one-night stay. Like many similar villages in these parts, the target market for accommodation owners was seemingly wealthy people on a weekend or short break that required a base for several days.

I'd managed to find accommodation at Corhampton Lane Farm a few miles south-west of the village, whose host, Suzanne, had offered to collect us from outside the Shoe Inn in Exton, if we called her on arrival there. We duly made the call and treated ourselves to a couple of coffees in the pub garden while we waited. Suzanne later ferried us to the pub and back for our evening meal and would return us there the next morning to resume our walk. Now that's what I call service and it was coupled with a comfortable stay at the farm.

During the evening, once back at the farm, Maureen checked the Country Walking Facebook Group that we use. As ever there were many messages of support from fellow walkers, plus more donations to our charity fundraising, for which we were immensely grateful. Interestingly several members of the group live within a reasonable distance of the SDW and were looking at opportunities to join us at some point. We also had a message from another Mont Blanc friend, Keren, who expected to join us the day after tomorrow.

The next morning Suzanne duly dropped us back at the Shoe Inn and we set off under overcast skies on another 12.5-mile walk, this time to the village of Buriton.

Just as in previous days, the paths were very good and great waymarking made navigation easy. At 2 miles, we reached a recommended view point, Old Winchester Hill. It was a clear day and this spot offered an unobstructed view through to the south coast and the rolling hills all around us. A mile or so further on we encountered what had thankfully been a relatively infrequent occurrence, crossing paths with real cows – real ones, that is! They were positioned directly on the footpath and were showing no signs of moving. We took our standard approach of watching them for a few minutes to determine how lively they were and, despite deciding they were calm, opted to take a detour round the perimeter of the pasture rather than attempt to walk through them. We got by with little interest shown on their part and, as is often the case, they never budged from their position. Always better to be safe than sorry though!

We stopped for an early coffee shortly afterwards at Whitewool Pond, a very peaceful fishing venue with a large wooden hut that serves as a reception area and cafe. The day had brightened up, with the sun now shining, so we decided to sit outside with a coffee and watch the few anglers present in their fruitless pursuit of whatever fish occupied the water. I can appreciate fishing in terms of the peace and tranquillity that goes with it, but personally I think it's less about sport and more about escapism from whatever hassles these guys in life.

After leaving the pond the excellent paths continued until we reached the interestingly named Sustainability Centre. It's predominantly a learning centre, working particularly with schools on a range of environmental awareness experiences. It also offers overnight stays in a yurt, which is a large tepee-like structure with a broad roof, often sleeping as many as six people. Nice and natural, but not for us I'm afraid.

The path peaked for the day at Butser Hill, enabling a view of the distant sea once more. A long descent over sweeping grassland took us down to the underpass below the busy A3 road, before rising on the other side of the road into the Queen Elizabeth Country Park. It was an unexpectedly steep trek through dense woods for a mile before we emerged into the sunlight via a lane. The SDW seldom passes through a village and Buriton, like many we'd be staying in, was a short distance off route. The lane sloped downhill, passing under a rail line, before entering the concise village. Just along the main street we found the Five Bells pub, our rendezvous place with Chris and Jane, who were sat outside enjoying a cool drink as we arrived. It was brilliant to see them again and the occasion was marked by our reaching exactly 900 miles at that point. After downing a couple of refreshing drinks ourselves, the four of us set off to lane-walk the 1.5 miles to our B&B, Nursted Farm.

It was a big, old farm building, full of character, with plenty of wood-lined walls and even an antique rocking horse in the hallway. Our hosts, Gordon and Mary, are the third generation of their family to run the farm, but they now focus on the B&B and leave the arduous farming work to the current and 4th generation, their son Andrew and his wife Elaine. Gordon and Mary, bless them, must have been in their late 70's or early 80's and ambled slowly up the sweeping stairs to take us to our rooms, which were decorated in keeping with the character of the farm. After we'd freshened up, Mary drove the four of us down to the pub for our evening meal, which was quite a nerve wracking experience even over that short distance. She couldn't collect us later, thankfully, so we opted for a taxi rather than a dark and wet walk back in the rain.

Breakfast was lovely the next morning, taken in the high-ceilinged dining room populated with traditional wooden furniture. It felt like the aged butler and housemaid were catering for us, as Gordon and Mary shuffled in and out of the room, back and forth to the kitchen. But they were lovely, gentle folk and overall it was a memorable place to stay.

We had been excitedly looking forward to walking with Chris and Jane. They became our very good friends when we walked the Mont Blanc massif with them in 2015. They met each other for the first time on a similar excursion to New Zealand some years earlier and became partners. Like us they're both retired from work and spend a lot of their time walking. We were delighted when they wanted to join us on the SDW. They'd previously walked the 2 days we'd just completed and would now walk with us to the end of the SDW at Eastbourne to complete the trail.

Initially we headed back towards Buriton a short way before picking up a bridleway that would soon link us up with the SDW for our 11.5 miles to Cocking. The track progressed through some unusually named places. After a stretch on the 'Milky Way', it rose to peak at 'Hundred Acres', which descended to 'Forty Acres Lane', to then nestle in The Bosom (I kid you not).

As we reached another Beacon Hill the extensive views became short lived as the sky darkened and rain arrived. At 6 miles heading towards us was Keren, who had parked at Cocking and walked out to meet us. She is always walking or travelling somewhere and is always on the go. It was still raining as we took lunch under the shelter of trees, sitting on a circle of moss-covered rocks like a group of overage adolescents on a Duke of Edinburgh challenge. All it lacked was a camp fire! After lunch, we hadn't walked far before the rain stopped and the views appeared again. Rolling hills, wooded areas, chalky paths, rabbit warrens, colourful arrays of wild flowers, blue skies dotted with white clouds, hay fields dancing in the breeze. It was so 'England's green and pleasant land', and immensely enjoyable to walk through.

At 10.5 miles, we reached the car park where Keren had left her car. She decided it was best if she drove up to Cocking and meet us at the B&B. We turned north off the SDW and followed a secluded path for the final mile until it joined the village street where our B&B, Moonlight Cottage was located. Keren was also staying over and the five of us had the place literally to ourselves, as our host lived in a house across the road. Once we'd all settled in we took the short walk to the local Blue Bell Pub, where we had a great evening reminiscing our Mont Blanc experiences and the other people we'd met on that trip. As a guided walk with a party of 16 together for 2 weeks, Mont Blanc was a very different experience to what Maureen and I had been experiencing on Caper, which for the most part had been just the two of us, on the road together for the past 10 weeks.

Breakfast the next morning felt just like 'old times', albeit they were only a year or so ago, with the five of us gathered together having a lively chat with a few jokes thrown in for good measure. Afterwards Keren took Maureen's rucksack to her car and then drove to the same car park as yesterday, while the remaining four of us set off to walk down to meet her there. Keren would be walking with us today for the first 5 miles before retracing her steps back to her car and then driving to meet us at our next B&B in Amberley, 12 miles away.

The day was warming up nicely as we headed up a gentle gradient, before it levelled out to reveal the classic Downs views that we were getting very used to enjoying. It was easy, straightforward walking in idyllic surroundings, plenty of wild flowers lining our chalky path, fields full of green grasses, broken occasionally by the golden shine of interspersed fields of barley. We took a long bag drop and nibbles break at 4 miles, sitting by a gate in a meadow for some final chit-chat before Keren's planned U-turn. The 5 miles point was duly reached, a sensible place for Keren to turn back as the path ahead would then dip downhill for a mile. And what goes down must come up, hence it climbed back up for a mile immediately afterwards. After scaling back to the modest height of 242 metres we felt a spot of lunch was called for, whilst enjoying the immense views. The sea was clearly in sight, along with a trio of suburban life populating the coastline, namely Bognor Regis, Littlehampton and Worthing.

The undulating path continued, dropping to reach a crossroads of paths before rising again to summit Bignor Hill. Here we came across Toby's Stone, a horseman's mounting block commemorating huntsman James Wentworth-Fitzwilliam, who somehow became known as Toby. Its three-tier shape, not unlike an Olympic Games podium, enabled each of us to stand proudly on their own step and entice a passer-by to kindly take a few photos. Huge open pastures filled the surrounding landscape, with visibility as far as the eye could see over vast swathes of countryside and an immense sky. There were dark clouds to our left, however, releasing a vertical shower of rain. The question was whether we could get our walk finished before it caught up with us.

At just over 11 miles we left the SDW and turned north along a quiet lane in search of our B&B, located in the village of Bury. The rain got to us, leading to a sudden doubling of our walking pace rather than go to the trouble of putting waterproofs on. Keren's car, parked outside Harkaway B&B, soon came into view. Our host Carol beckoned everyone in and soon whipped up tea, coffee and homemade cake – just the job. An hour later we recovered Maureen's rucksack from Keren's car as we said our goodbyes to her. It had been great to see her again and we were also very grateful for her support.

That evening we walked to the recommended local pub, the Squire and Horse. We found a table, bought drinks and ordered food, then waited, and waited, and waited, and waited! People were coming to other tables, eating and leaving while we were still waiting. The staff kept promising our food was on its way, but we weren't seeing anything. The waitress offered us a round of drinks on the house while we waited. Eventually I asked to see the manager, who was upstairs in his residence. He came along, very apologetic, but unusually blamed his junior chef who had used the wrong oven, causing a long cooking time to be needed. He offered us free deserts by way of recompense, which we decided to have on the basis of walking them off tomorrow. Of course, we omitted to mention that we'd also had free drinks and when we got the bill there were no drinks at all shown. So, whilst the wait was unacceptable, two rounds of free drinks and free deserts persuaded us not to negatively review the pub on Trip Advisor!

Back at the B&B we received messages via the Country Walking Facebook Group to confirm that Sally Oakley-Qajar and

Becky Wells would be meeting up with us in the morning at an agreed rendezvous point. Our good fortune with rucksack movers continued, with Jacqueline Gale confirming she would collect one from us tomorrow and take it on to our next B&B, she would then walk back along the SDW towards us to meet up with everyone. Suddenly our group of four had become seven. How marvellous to have such support.

We awoke the next morning excited for several reasons. It was day 71, just 8 walking days to go before we'd be standing triumphantly on the top of Dover Castle (we hoped) in exactly a week's time. We were also looking forward to the day's 13.5 mile walk to Upper Beeding, plus we'd meet for the first time three friends we only knew through the online world.

Breakfast was just ending when Jacqueline joined us. After a few minutes of getting to know each other she was keen to get on her way to Upper Beeding, deliver the rucksack and start walking in our direction. Soon afterwards Chris, Jane, Maureen and I were retracing our lane walk of late yesterday to re-join the SDW.

A couple of fields led us to a metal footbridge over the river, followed by the path dipping under a rail track. We then crossed a lane to re-join the now familiar chalk path. As we walked uphill we could see two figures at the top waving frantically to us, unmistakably Sally and Becky. It's always a strange occurrence to meet people that we've known online for the past 10 weeks, who we've dialogued with but not spoken to directly, whose online photos makes it feel like we know them, yet this is the first direct contact. They were both very bubbly individuals, very easy to chat with and exchange walking experiences (first things first, after all) before finding out lots more about them, where they lived, where they worked etc.

As in previous days, the views were spectacular. The thing that really took our breath was the sheer distance that could be seen, easily 30 miles in every direction, probably more. The sky was vast, fabulous clouds creating a snow-white blanket above us, but not blocking out the warm sunshine. The first 5 miles were similar to a ridge walk, enabling views in all directions. To the south the sea seemed to be getting ever closer. The landscape was scattered with rolling fields of wheat or grass swaying in the breeze. To the north more glorious countryside, injected with villages every now and then baring rhythmically similar names such as Storrington, Ashington and Washington.

A now familiar figure was heading towards us in the distance. Jacqueline had made great progress and reached us at 5.5 miles. Soon we crossed the busy dual carriageway that is the A24 and headed uphill to stop for lunch at Chanctonbury Ring, a prehistoric hill fort atop Chanctonbury Hill. What remains today is a roughly circular low earthen rampart surrounded by a ditch, which provides a great stopping point for a typical picnic in the countryside. Our group was one of several enjoying the peace and tranquillity, enhanced by the occasional horse riders trotting by, day visitors with their dogs enjoying some freedom from their leashes, 1 or 2 joggers and a couple of mountain bikers. The SDW really is a trail that everyone can enjoy.

From our lofty (for these parts) position, barely breaking 200 metres in height, it was mostly downhill for the remainder of the walk. The views were very similar to the morning's walk, yet there was no chance of ever tiring of this landscape. It was a walker's heaven, wonderful scenery, effortless walking and a day that shouldn't ever have ended. At 10 miles, though there was a surprise in store for us. There on Annington Hill was the biggest pig farm I've ever seen. The smell reached us quite a way before we encountered the first pig pens. It wasn't too nauseating, but after the day we'd had it was such a contrast. There were hundreds of free-roaming pigs between a multitude of pens, though a thin electrified wire separated us from them. The SDW went right through the farm, which was basically the hillside strewn with pigs. I must say that the residents looked very happy with their scenic homestead.

Once past the grunting mass the path further descended to meet up with a river. It was time to take our customary end-of-day leave of the SDW and head north along the riverbank to locate our B&B in Upper Beeding. We said our goodbyes to Sally, Becky and Jacqueline, but, it was only au revoir, as they would all be meeting up with us again in the morning. Chris and Jane had enjoyed getting to know the others and we had all got on well. It had been a truly memorable day.

"I've got a problem", Maureen said, soon after waking up the next morning. "Both my feet hurt, and they're swollen. I might not be able to walk today".

"Oh no", I exclaimed. "Let's get something cold on them and it might reduce the swelling". I went to the en-suite and soaked a towel in cold water, then draped it across her feet. "They don't look too bad", I said, trying desperately to think of something positive to say about this potential show stopper.

"They really hurt, God knows why, they were okay when I went to bed", Maureen said.

"It might be because you've walked 900-odd miles, or because it was hot yesterday, or both", I said. "Maybe they'll feel okay once your boots are on, giving them some support", I suggested, knowing it was probably a stupid thing to say, or nonsense, or both! Maureen eased them on, cursing and groaning as she did with the disappointment and pain, but determined to get them on, gently tying the laces.

"I'll just have to see how it goes", she said. We had a long 18 miles ahead of us to Kingston-Near-Lewes. Why can't these things happen on a shorter 'rest' day? Hopefully once underway her feet might feel better, or with the help of our walking companions we'd take her mind of them.

We set off on a brisk climb, the first of many we'd encounter on today's undulating route. The OS map was dense with contours, indicating the rise and fall of the land, but it also showed that many areas of land in these parts were known as a 'Bottom' – Mossy, Bushy, Hazelholt, Whitelot, Ewe and Rag to name but a few. As planned we met Sally, Becky and Jacqueline at the 2 miles point outside Tottington Barn Youth Hostel. Maureen felt duty bound to mention her feet issue, but said they'd felt reasonably okay so far, so she was optimistic of completing the day.

It was another beautiful morning, the wide-open expanses of the Downs looking dramatic and impressive in the sunlight. An early coffee break was taken at 4 miles, to sit and enjoy the views across Adder Bottom, whilst chatting predominantly about walking. Sally, Becky and Jacqueline, like us, were all doing the Country Walking Facebook Group challenge to complete 1,000 miles during the calendar year and were progressing well.

"It's alright for you", Sally said, "You're getting your 1,000 miles done in one go".

"Absolutely", I replied, "You should try it".

The miles passed by with the incredible scenery unrelenting. The sweeping Fulking Escarpment (yes, really!) we were walking across slopped down to our left to a valley that swept north to the distant skyline, where it met the blue sky peppered with occasional white clouds. It was the kind of view that you could stop and just look at all day long. However, as the day shifted into the afternoon the clouds joined to become one, blocking any sunshine, but without the threat of rain. Maureen was walking okay and through the welcome distraction of our party of walkers

I think her mind was largely taken off thinking about her feet. It might have been a different story if it had been just the two of us walking today.

A lunch break was taken at 9 miles, overlooking Denclier Bottom, and beyond to Brighton and Hove on the coast, now just 6 miles to the south of us as the crow flies. It really did feel like we were graduating down to the sea, though it would be another 30 miles before we reached it. Today's path had so far headed primarily eastwards, but just after 12 miles it took a sharp right turn to steer due south for a couple of miles, crossing a bridge over the busy A27 road. Once across we faced a steep climb through a long pasture, inhabited by a sizable herd of cows. Fortunately, they were well used to walkers on the SDW and paid us little attention, as we nervously glided past them.

We left the SDW with half a mile to go to drop steeply into Kingston, where we soon located our accommodation for the night, Nightingales B&B. Sally, Becky and Jacqueline had organised themselves with car shuffling, such that they had Jacqueline's car at the B&B for them all to head back westwards, picking up Sally and Becky's cars on route. We were very grateful for the efforts they'd put in to be part of our journey and sad to be saying goodbye to them. Maureen had made it despite her feet problems and when she took her boots off there was no sign of swelling, so hopefully they'd be fine in the morning too.

Our host Jean made us very welcome in her immaculate property. After freshening up we checked our messages and to our surprise and delight another 'rucksack angel' had offered to call at the B&B in the morning to collect Maureen's rucksack and take it on to our next port of call, Alfriston. It had been another great day on the SDW and we chatted about it constantly on our way to eat at the nearby pub 'The Juggs'.

213

An early morning knock on our bedroom door, just as we were getting ready, was followed by Jean's gentle voice.

"Nicola has arrived and is waiting in the breakfast room for you", she announced.

"Thanks, Jean, we'll be there in just a moment", Maureen replied. Once dressed, we made our way to the breakfast area to find Nicola chatting with Jean. Chris and Jane soon joined us. We were all slightly taken aback to see that she was wearing a nurse's uniform. We exchanged greetings.

"It's great to see you. Are you heading for work?" I asked.

"No, I've just done a 12-hour night shift at the local hospital. It's nearer for me to collect your rucksack now on my way home and I'll deliver it first, as I'll need to go to bed during the daytime", she replied.

"How amazing of you to come to see us and to help us, after working all night. It's so fantastic of you to do this", I exclaimed. To think that we were all total strangers, but here she was helping us on our way with such a great act of kindness.

"It's no problem. I'd also like to meet up with you one day soon to walk some of the way. I'll text you to confirm the where and when", she replied.

"That would be great, we'll look forward to it", Maureen said.

In a matter of minutes Nicola had left with the rucksack. On this occasion, it wouldn't be the last time that we would see our Good Samaritan. But for the four of us today it was a 12 mile walk to Alfriston, our penultimate day on the SDW. It looked to be quite a challenging day ahead of us, trending downhill for the first 5 miles, then uphill for 4 miles before down again for the final 3 miles.

We knew from the ending of yesterday's walk that today would start with an initial steep climb out of Kingston to re-join the SDW. We soon worked off our comprehensive breakfast. The sun was already high in the sky and as soon as we gained a little height the immense views opened once more. The excellent paths that had formed most of the route so far continued, including a long section through crop fields that was more like a concrete road in appearance. Soon after this we came across a wooden signpost, similar to a footpath finger post, but shaped like a cross. It depicted the Meridian Line, with the left-hand arm pointing to the western hemisphere and the right-hand arm pointing to the eastern hemisphere. This post is also known as the Bradley Meridian Line, which is positioned 6 metres to the west of the Prime Meridian Line, which passes through Greenwich near London. However, that line has now been assessed as being in the wrong place too and should be 334 feet to the east of where it currently is. Will the true Meridian Line please stand up!

The temperature was reaching the mid-20's as we dropped down to the small hamlet of Southease, which was notable for its impressive church with an unusual circular Saxon tower. Soon we crossed a bridge over the River Ouse. From this point the river would only need to snake south for 4 miles before it entered the English Channel at Newhaven Harbour.

Once across the river and over a nearby train track, the path led us to the Southease Youth Hostel Association campus, where we decided a break for drinks and a light refuelling would be in order. It was a pleasant enough place to sit outside and enjoy a break, but had we known that the speed of service – or lack of it – would extend our 10 minutes stop to 40 minutes we may well have chosen to keep walking.

Eventually, after some frustration, we could get back to our walk to start the long uphill stretch. We soon encountered a herd of cows who had taken up residence at the side of the footpath. We had little choice but to pass within touching distance of them. They must have been well used to SDW walkers as they let us go through without any problem. The ascent in the heat was taking its toll, but at 7 miles we reached the radio station masts indicated on the OS map, which were at just too good a spot not to take our lunch break. Chris and Jane were in good spirits as we sat there 'putting the world to rights' on any number of issues whilst we ate our snacks. It had been brilliant having their company on the SDW for what will have been a week by the end of the next day's walk, but then they'd leave us, and we would so miss them.

We set off again and immediately came upon a huge hillside that was a carpet of tall yellow buttercups intermixed with large white daisies. The landscape was an array of colour, from the golden fields of wheat and barley, to the green pastures, the sand coloured dips, the blues and pinks of numerous different wild flowers and the vast blue sky with cotton wool clouds floating slowly by. It was one of those English summer days to savour, one on which you could happily continue to walk until the very last drop of sun disappeared. We eventually reached Long Barrow viewpoint, situated at the day's highest point of 217 metres and giving amazing views in all directions.

To our left we could see Alfriston nestled in the valley some 4 miles ahead of us. The long descent to reach it then began and unusually the SDW took us right into the village. We arrived mid-afternoon, the sun now beating down on us, the village centre feeling quite humid as we made our way down the main road to find our B&B, Ye Olde Smugglers Inne.

"We're going to sit outside somewhere and have a drink", Jane said.

"Okay, we'll go and check us all in", I replied, innocently unaware of the saga that was about to unravel. We approached the bar.

"Hello, it's Mr & Mrs Shipley. I have two rooms booked, one for us and the other for our friends Chris and Jane", I confirmed. The on-duty member of staff retrieved the accommodation register to verify our details.

"I only have you down for one room", she said.

"No, it's definitely two", I said, producing both my email confirmation on my mobile and a paper copy. "I also telephoned last night to verify when we'd be arriving and to confirm that a rucksack would be delivered for us during today".

"It was two rooms, but it's been changed to one", she said, with increasing embarrassment.

I was starting to get irritated. "I'm not interested if it's been changed, I've got a confirmed booking. Could you get the manager for me, please?" I said.

She made a call and a few minutes later the manager appeared, and the situation was related to her.

"You're right it should be two rooms. Someone has checked–in earlier and convinced my member of staff to amend their booking from a one room to two. I'll remove them", she said with an air of authority.

The offending couple had dropped their bags in 'our' room and gone off to a local wedding. To our surprise the manager grabbed their bags and the few things they'd hung up and took them out of the room.

"There you go, sorry about that", she said.

"The only problem is that they've obviously got a room key and will be coming back, no doubt quite late, expecting to get into this room", I advised.

"Well that's their problem", she said, dismissively.

"No, it isn't, it's yours. I'm not having arguments with a no-doubt well intoxicated couple at 3am or whatever time in the morning they get back, hammering on the door to this room. It's your problem and you need to sort it out with them when they turn up", I insisted. She wasn't happy, but accepted that it did fall on her to follow this through. To compound the issue, there was no additional way to secure the room door and they could open the door with their key even if I locked it.

We ate in that night and the main topic of conversation with Chris and Jane was the room saga. We retired reasonably early in the hope of getting some sleep before the expected fireworks started when the wedding goers returned. We weren't wrong! I'd taken the precaution of wedging a chair under the room door handle in case a forced entry was attempted. We got to sleep okay, but in the early hours raised voices woke us up and no doubt everybody else staying there. A battle of words between the manager and the unknown couple, with plenty of commotion as presumably bags were moved and alternative sleeping arrangements determined, which went on for a good hour before things quietened down again. Our door security was not put to the test, thankfully.

The next morning, we somewhat sheepishly went down to breakfast and exchanged the night's experiences with Chris and Jane. Others were having breakfast, but we had no way of knowing who the displaced couple were. Afterwards when we checked out the manager tried to cover herself by putting the blame for the mix up on the online booking system.

"I think the problem occurred when the other couple checked-in. The register should not have been changed, however profusely the other couple might have said they had two rooms booked, as they wouldn't have been able to evidence it. Everything that happened subsequently, including your night-time arguments, have been as a result of that", I suggested. I wasn't a happy chappy and was more than pleased to get out of there.

Today's walk was one I'd been looking forward to since I first put it into the overall route plan. It was the final day on the SDW and, while in one sense we'd all be dismayed to be finishing it, we were excited at the prospect of walking over the famous white cliffs that are the Seven Sisters. There are two routes for completing the SDW from Alfriston. There's a clockwise route that heads due east before turning south to approach Eastbourne from the north. My preferred route was the anti-clockwise route, going due south to the coast and then turning east to approach Eastbourne from the west, via the Seven Sisters. Why the route splits into two from Alfriston I still haven't discovered!

We left Maureen's rucksack at the B&B as the wonderful Nicola had offered to collect it later in the day and take it on to Eastbourne. She also confirmed that she would walk part of the way from Eastbourne to Hastings with us the following day, which Maureen and I were already looking forward to.

All that stood between us and Eastbourne was a 12-mile walk. The weather was perfect, nice and warm with a slight breeze. The four of us headed through the narrow back streets of Alfriston to pick up our path next to the River Cuckmere and follow this for the first mile. This led onto a couple of open fields from where we could see to our left the Alfriston White Horse carved into the hillside. A delightful stretch through woods ensued, before we reached the village of Exceat. This resides against the very busy A259. There were hordes of people there, evidently a key stopping place for day trippers looking to walk the Seven Sisters. There's a visitor's centre and two large car parks and it felt like we'd been plucked out of the quiet countryside and dropped into the paved street of a popular shopping area.

It was a challenge just crossing the A259 as the traffic was unrelenting in both directions, so Chris resorted to holding an arm aloft like a traffic policeman. Once across there were two ant trails of people heading for the coast, those on a lower path leading to the beach and others on our intended path, which gradually rose to the hill top. We could already see the undulating white face of the cliffs stretching away into the distance, supporting a broad carpet of green pastures heading into the distance like a roller-coaster ride. It was truly awe inspiring. Somehow it made me feel very patriotic and proud of this renowned area of the English coast.

The Seven Sisters are individually named and from west to east are Haven Brow, Short Brow, Rough Brow, Brass Point, Flagstaff Point, Flat Hill and Baily's Hill. In recent times, an eighth sister has 'appeared' due to sea erosion of the chalk cliffs, named Went Hill Brow. The hills would be a tough end to the SDW, rising steeply to each summit and then descending significantly after each one. These dips are also individually named, generally taking each sister's name but followed by that common occurrence in these parts: 'Bottom'. If I was the landscape I don't know if I'd prefer to be a Short Bottom or a Rough Bottom!

We were so thankful for the glorious weather, which is just what any walker on these hills would wish for to see them in all their glory. There were numerous people out walking in each direction, family groups, couples and many individuals clearly meeting a personal walking, running or cycling challenge. There was even the official finishing point of a running event on one hill, festooned with bunting and flags. The white cliffs looked magnificent, gigantic and impressive, yet sometimes delicate looking as if fragments of them might crumble into the sea at any moment.

Just after our halfway mark we reached Birling Gap, the first access point inland by road since we joined the hills, and therefore again very busy with people. It was the ideal place for a lunch stop with plenty of facilities there, so we sat in the sun eating and watching the world go by, observing the different ways people were enjoying their day out. A peculiar metal staircase encased in an oblong metal tower took people vertically down from the cliff top to the beach some 30 metres below, from where a plethora of beach 'noises' were emanating – waves crashing on the beach, the laughter of children playing, the occasional dog barking.

The magnificent views continued after we resumed and soon we came to the notable landmark of the Belle Tout lighthouse. Built in 1832, it was the original lighthouse for that stretch of coast until it was decommissioned in 1902. It then changed private ownership many times, eventually becoming a B&B. Due to the ongoing erosion of the coastline, in 1999 the lighthouse was physically moved inland by 56 feet using some incredible engineering techniques.

A long surge uphill took us to the viewpoint at Beachy Head. The lighthouse here sits below at sea level, sited about 165 metres seawards from the base of the cliffs. It is known for its distinctive red-and-white striped tower and is an impressive sight against the blue of the sea. Our walk over the 'eighth' sisters ended here, with the path now heading steeply downhill towards the finish, with panoramic views over Eastbourne. After a tricky last few metres down a grassy bank we reached the official SDW finishing post, located outside the simply named 'The Kiosk' cafe, where we took the obligatory photos of our success. All that remained was the final 2 miles to our B&B, Sea Beach House, probably named by the owners while looking out of their front windows!

We crossed the road from The Kiosk to head down Dukes Drive towards the sea front, instantly accompanied by cars, pedestrians, schools, houses and all the usual trappings of being back in a town. After several hours on the rolling green hills of the SDW it was quite a contrast, but not an unpleasant one. Eastbourne struck me as a tidy, probably middle-class resort, which would not permit amusement arcades, candy floss and tacky souvenirs to be fronted on its esplanade. The sea was only a few metres below us now as we continued along King Edward's Parade, lined by gardens edged with palm trees and cactus, not natives of the area I imagined, but adding a tropical feel to things. After passing more regimental seaside flower beds we reached the inevitable pier, no-doubt Victorian, as that was the era fascinated enough by the prospect of walking out over the sea to build them. A little further on and we arrived at Sea Beach House. All of us were ready for a break, having had a great final day on the SDW, but desperately needing to freshen up and go out to eat.

After a celebratory meal at a recommended local Indian restaurant, Maureen and I returned to the B&B, while Chris and Jane opted to enjoy the last evening of their holiday visiting a few local hostelries...and why not? For them their walk was over. For us, we had to keep relatively clear heads for the final push to Dover, now just 4 days away.

Chapter 12 – We Can Make It

We awoke the next morning with a realisation of the significance of the day. It was Monday 18th July, day 75 of our long-distance walk and the start of the last section of our journey. Eastbourne was a key point on the route, the end of the amazing South Downs Way and the beginning of a 61-mile coastal stretch to Dover. We were facing our 'final frontier' with excitement and some trepidation too. Could we do it, will our luck in having no injuries and few health or fitness problems continue? We had come so far, 980 miles down the length of the country. Just 4 more days of walking and we'd be there, journey's end.

"How are you this morning, babe?" I asked, as we dressed before heading down to breakfast.

"I'm okay, looking forward to it", Maureen replied, enthusiastically. "My only concern is the weather forecast, which says the temperature will reach 28 degrees today".

"We'll ensure we have plenty of water and sunscreen, and pray for a sea breeze, plus some shade along the way", I said. "If we take breaks every 3 miles and keep the pace steady, I'm sure we'll be okay", I said, with genuine optimism. We had 15 miles to walk to Hastings. Route finding should be a doddle, we just needed to keep the sea on our right and we were bound to be heading east!

Whilst we would be saying our goodbyes to Chris and Jane this morning, we wouldn't be alone for long. Our virtual friends on the Country Walking Facebook Group had been in touch. Bev Wood had offered to do a rucksack transfer for us and would also walk the first few miles to the edge of town. Nicola Godin would meet us shortly afterwards and walk about 8 miles with us, so plenty of support to keep us going.

Chris and Jane had been brilliant in walking with us for 7 days. It had been immense fun, a great experience and filled with memories, but sadly they had to head home. No sooner had they 'exited to our right' than Bev 'entered from our left'. It was almost as if we were the star attraction of this seaside show, with one support act leaving and the next one joining us on stage. We dropped Maureen's rucksack into Bev's car and then we were off. It was only just after 9am, but the sun was already hot.

After a short distance along the promenade we veered off to the right to join a cycle path that ran behind the beach. The curve in the coastline soon gave us great views back over the sea towards Eastbourne, with a glimpse of the white cliffs beyond the town. The promenade led us down to Sovereign Harbour. Bev's local knowledge came in very useful here in guiding us over a series of small footbridges through the newly developed marina. The large expanse of water fronting the marina was surrounded by a variety of waterside apartments, overseeing whatever nautical vessels eased past them and out to sea. Sailing boats of different shapes and sizes packed the marina, their tall masts upright like a succession of flagpoles. Evidently a lot of thought had been put into the design and shape of the whole area to make it a very pleasing and attractive place to live, though no doubt a very expensive one!

At this point we said our goodbyes to Bev who left us to walk back to her car. As in earlier instances, it was strangely surreal to meet someone for the first time, spend an hour or so with them and then they were gone.

Once clear of the harbour the cycle path turned inland, and our coastal path withered to a narrow footpath. As it did so we passed the first of many Martello Towers, small, circular defensive forts that were built along the coastline during the 19th century. They look quite round and squat, yet are 40 feet high and typically held

15-25 armed men. The path soon ended on reaching the shingle beach, where we similarly turned inland down an access drive to a caravan park. This led us to the main A259 road where after a mile in the company of light traffic we were joined by Nicola, just as we reached Pevensey Bay. It was lovely to see her again, this time dressed in lightweight summer gear and sandals ready for our walk together. Nicola and her family have lived in the area for many years and she was able to give us interesting snippets of information along the way. In planning this part of the route, I had hoped we'd be able to walk along the beach, but Nicola advised us that it was mostly shingle for another mile or so and would be hard going. There was no footpath, so we opted to stay with the road. Fortunately, the A259 headed north before long and we could transfer to a minor road that ran near the coast.

Soon we came across examples of that unique aspect of the English seaside, beach huts. As you'd expect they were in an array of colours, but what surprised us was the variety in sizes that we saw here and further along towards Hastings. Instead of a standard garden shed size, some were twice as deep, others had extra windows, and some had a patch of land with them too. As we continued it seemed that the more we progressed towards Hastings the larger the beach huts became.

The temperature continued to rise and by now we were ready for a break and some shade, which so far had been totally lacking on this coastal route. At Norman's Bay, we decided to head inland to where Nicola knew the Star Inn would be waiting for us like an oasis in a desert. Pints of ice cold lime and lemonade were what was needed and were soon being consumed beneath a sun canopy in the pub's garden. It was an effort to leave that shady spot, both because it was a hugely enjoyable place to be on a hot afternoon and because we knew the sun would beat down on us again as soon as we ventured out. Before leaving the owner kindly refilled our water bottles with chilled water.

Boy, it was hot as we walked a minor lane through Cooden Beach, where Nicola pointed out a house reputedly owned by TV and radio celebrity Graham Norton. No-one appeared to be at home or we might have offered him the chance of an interview for his show! A beach promenade made a welcome return at Cooden town, enabling traffic-free walking again in a light breeze coming off the sea. The town had taken the initiative to build artistically shaped, but very effective, large sun shelters, one of which we gleefully stopped at for a break to eat our packed lunches. Afterwards the lovely Nicola had to leave us to take a bus back to Pevensey Bay, where her car was parked.

With 10 of the 15 miles completed there was still 2 to 3 hours of walking to be done. In a matter of minutes back out in the sun we were both pouring with sweat. The day was proving to be a scorcher, and this was not a heat we'd normally be walking in, but we had to soldier on to the finish come what may. Despite starting off with four bottles of water and having refilled them along the way, we were getting down to our last half bottle. We soon reached Bexhill, still on the promenade, where there was another long line of various coloured beach huts. The beach itself was devoid of people, just the odd one or two taking a paddle in the cool sea. The only shade to be seen was under the sun brolly protecting the happily unemployed life guard sitting atop a white umpire's chair. There wasn't a ship in sight on the sea and the sky was undisturbed by air traffic. It was seemingly too hot for anyone to do anything, except for two crazy walkers!

At 13 miles Maureen began to really feel the heat. She was walking on autopilot as we reached the outskirts of Hastings, longing to stop but knowing that if she did there was a good chance that would be it for the day. I too was barely coping with the heat but felt I must 'lead from the front' and voiced encouragement to hopefully ensure we both made it. The outskirts of a town can often lead to a false sense of security, suggesting that the walk for the day is almost over, whereas there was still a long stretch to do to reach our hotel. As we entered the High Street, with its well-manicured flower beds, Maureen was desperate to get out of the sun and dipped into the first hotel we came upon to gain some respite. We took a 15 minutes break there, freshened up as best we could by washing our faces in their facilities, before making the final half mile stint to our own hotel. We arrived there at 4.30pm, but Maureen by now was not feeling too well at all. We both drank what seemed like gallons of water and then showered, before Maureen took to lying on the bed to recover.

"There's no way I can go out to eat tonight", she said.

"We need some food, though, so I'll fetch some from a local supermarket", I said. As much as I felt shattered, I did feel okay to make the pilgrimage to the nearby shops, where I picked up an array of healthy food for our dinner-a-la-bed!

Breakfast television the next morning confirmed our worst fears. The day would be even hotter than yesterday, with the south-east corner of the UK weather map showing a very deep red colour, with a round symbol displaying '30'. Under normal circumstances a July day with this kind of weather would be wonderful, but when facing a 12 mile walk to Rye along the exposed south coast only one thought came to mind...we were going to melt!

Before the real walking got underway we had an unusual start to the day to look forward to. Andrew White from the Country Walking Facebook Group had been in touch a few days previously to arrange to meet us in Hastings. He had offered both to take a rucksack on to our next B&B at Dymchurch and to give us a guided walk as we passed through Hastings to head east. We in turn offered to buy him breakfast in a local cafe, as our hotel, like most of those on the sea front, didn't provide it.

Andrew was waiting for us in the lobby, his beaming smile greeting us along with a firm handshake, as we made our exit to the oven awaiting us outside. The heat hit us as soon as we stepped out onto the pavement. What a scorcher.

"Hi Andrew, it's great to meet you and thank you for showing us through your town", I said as we walked along the promenade.

"It's my pleasure. I've lived here for many years and love the place and its history", he replied.

Of course, from our school days the mere mention of Hastings immediately makes us think of the year 1066 and the Battle of Hastings. This involved the Norman-French invaders of William, the Duke of Normandy and the Anglo-Saxon army under King Harold Godwinson. It's regarded as the beginning of the Norman conquest of England. The fighting took place in a field 7.5 mile north-west of Hastings, where the town of Battle now stands. Andrew's tour would pass less violent landmarks as we headed into the 'Old Town' to find a cafe.

The ruins of Hastings Castle could be seen high up to our left as we skirted through streets full of character, just behind the more traditional looking sea front. Here we dropped into the first cafe open for business and, after a healthy but generous breakfast, we continued our tour at the harbour. Many small fishing vessels had been pulled out of the water onto the beach by small tractors, following their early morning return to the harbour with their catch. Nearby were the tall, thin fish net huts, painted black, and up to 3 storeys high. Established in 1835, they are unique to Hastings and are the traditional storage buildings of the Hastings fishing fleet. They were used to stow gear made from natural materials such as cotton nets, hemp ropes and canvas sails, which would rot if left in the open, especially when wet. Thirty-nine of them are now Grade 2 Listed Buildings. We never realised there was so much to see in Hastings and we committed to returning one day when we weren't on a mission.

We walked past the East Cliff funicular railway that claws its way up the hillside, to take the same stiff climb using a flight of steps. Once on the cliff top we enjoyed panoramic views over the town, including towards the local amateur theatre where Andrew has performed a variety of acting and operational roles over many years. Just after 2 miles we reached Andrew's turnaround point. It had been interesting to meet him and share his enthusiasm for just some of the places of interest in this historic town. Before he departed he presented us with a badge each, making us honorary members of his walking group, 'Team South East'.

As we headed steeply downhill a temporary sign advised "Warning – Landslide – Path Closed". Moments later, however, two walkers came up towards us.

"It's passable with care", one of them confirmed.

We cautiously continued and soon came to a section where the whole path had fallen away. We clambered down while holding onto the branches of a bent tree, inching our way through a mixture of broken branches and bracken, ensuring our footing was secure with each step. It was slow progress for about 50 metres until the unaffected part of the path was reached again.

I hadn't expected any landslips on our route, assuming that any that had occurred would be cliff edges going into the sea and not where we'd be walking. I also hadn't expected to be heading downhill, as in my route planning I took this section to be similar to going along the cliffs on the SDW. On the back climb up Maureen developed significant breathing difficulties, being slightly asthmatic, and at one point I feared she would pass out. She was breathing very heavily and was visibly shaky. It was no place to have problems, buried in the bracken halfway up a hill.

Thankfully, I managed to pull her up with a guiding hand until we eventually emerged onto the hill top and an open, flat landscape once more. We'd only gone half a mile in over an hour. This would inevitably prolong the walk, not something either of us needed in the heat.

We were now on the Saxon Shore Way, a 163-mile-long distance path that runs as far as Gravesend in Kent. We would be walking on this for two of our last three days, but tomorrow it turns inland to head north rather than sticking to the coast. The views out to sea were amazing, a rich blue sky hanging over a calm and glistening mass of water. But it was short lived at this point as we soon entered a wooded stretch that formed Hastings Country Park. Route finding was proving uncertain, but fortunately a guy came along whom we asked for directions.

"You're on the right track, just take a left at the next junction and keep going", he said.

"Many thanks", we replied. "Are you heading anywhere in particular?" I asked.

"I'm going down to the bay below. It's very secluded and the best place around here for a dip in the sea", he said.

"Sounds great, we must look it up the next time we're in these parts. Enjoy your swim", I said.

As we went our separate ways we thought no more of our encounter, until shortly afterwards another guy materialised. We exchanged pleasantries without really stopping, but he did tell us that he, too, was heading for Covehurst Bay, for a skinny dip! Again, it all seemed entirely feasible on a hot day, but when a third guy came our way heading in the same direction we began to get more curious.

"It's a great spot down there", he said to us, "You should go", he said, seemingly looking more in my direction than Maureen's. It was then that the penny dropped, later confirmed when we had a pub stop, that this bay was a men-only naturist spot!

By midday, after 5 miles of 'unusual' walking experiences and significant heat, we reached Fairlight Cove. We stopped at the local pub, 'The Cove', desperately in need of an ice-cold drink. It was a celebratory drink as it was here that we reached our 1,000-mile point! We decided to also take lunch there, ostensibly to have a period out of the sun, as we had no idea where future shade opportunities might be, if anywhere. The barman kindly refilled our water bottles with chilled water before we found the will to step outside into the blazing sun. We both had sun hats, of course, and were well covered in factor 30 sun screen, but these didn't prevent us oozing with sweat walking in such a sauna.

We had 3 miles to do to reach Winchelsea, with our route turning inland after the first mile to walk alongside the Royal Military Canal. As we laboured across the final three pastures the heat was bouncing up off the ground as if we were pavement walking rather than being on dry mud and grass. We'd never endured such conditions on any of our previous walks and it was certainly taking its toll on both of us. Our water was depleting rapidly as our path joined the main road at Winchelsea. The pub indicated on the map, a potential refuge from the elements, had long since permanently closed, with no other options we could see for getting out of the sun.

Our energy levels were very low by now, but we needed to bite the bullet and get through the final 2 miles to our destination of Rye. A short stretch of lane walking led to a footpath that shadowed the busy main road all the way there. The 2 miles were completed entirely on autopilot and in all honesty, we both struggle to remember them. It was simply a case of getting it done, find our B&B, 'The Old Borough Arms', and get out of the sun to start our recovery. Thankfully when we arrived at the B&B their check-in procedure was simple and quick. We were shown to our room where we were delighted to get our boots and socks off our radiating feet, plus the rest of our gear, and begin the cooling down process. Long stints in a cool shower followed, but as we relaxed, sat upright on the bed, we soon began to feel hot again. It was going to be an uncomfortable night and there was no air conditioning. But first we needed to eat. I'd spotted a nice looking Italian restaurant on the way into Rye and convinced Maureen that we needed to make the effort to go there and fill up on pasta. And very nice it was too! We felt much better afterwards.

That evening back at the B&B we watched the weather forecast for the next day. More hot weather was expected, but a few degrees lower, thankfully, and probably an overcast start to the day. We had a long walk of 16.5 miles to Dymchurch to complete, our penultimate day of this epic journey.

"There's no-way I'll be able to carry a full rucksack", Maureen exclaimed.

"There's only one thing for it then, I'll get a taxi to take it to Dymchurch for us", I said. That was so much easier said than done. There is a dearth of taxi firms in the Rye area. Only six were listed, of which three never answered their telephone and two others had stopped taxiing. My final option needed some persuading.

"I can do it, but it'll have to be early as I'm supposed to be on holiday", he said.

"You can make it as early as you wish, I'm sure I'll be up", I replied. It turned out that his definition of early was 8am! It was, though, the most expensive ride ever taken by a rucksack, I would think, as he charged the princely sum of £38! In an obscure way, it was good value for money, under the circumstances.

We were up with the larks the next morning, not having slept too well in the heat. Maureen discovered that she had a heat rash where you wouldn't really want one. Without being indelicate, it was somewhere between her waist and the top of her thighs. We treated it with what we had, which wasn't much. We knew we couldn't get anything else as the local shops wouldn't be open until after 9am. After a quick breakfast, I met the taxi driver outside as arranged and passed the rucksack over to him. It was warm, but the overcast sky was keeping the heat at bay for the moment, so I was eager to get as many miles done as we could before things really hotted up.

First up was a short walk through the cobbled back streets of Rye that brought us to its medieval town wall, incorporating an arched gateway. I stopped to record my usual morning video clip introducing the day. I pointed the camera in Maureen's direction.

"Can I just say for the record that I have sore lips, sore 'other bits', my ankles are swollen and I'm exhausted", she said.

It was going to be hard to keep her in a positive frame of mind today, but with just 2 days to go I was confident she'd make it. As for me, I was feeling weary, maybe psychologically because I knew we were approaching journey's end and possibly because it was the 77th consecutive day of walking!

Once through the gateway the lane dropped down to a bridge over the river, after which we joined a cycle track that would take us the first 3 miles to Camber. The town instantly strikes you as a seaside holiday resort. It makes most of its income from visitors to the vast Camber Sands, which is indeed sandy rather than the shingle that has populated all other stretches of beach so far on this coastline. Towards the town centre we passed the entrance to

Pontins Holiday Camp, a traditional UK holiday experience that still seems to thrive. There was a steady trickle of holidaymakers coming out of the camp gates and crossing the road heading for a day by the sea. It was quite misty at this point and very windy, a complete change to yesterday's climate. Wind breakers would be needed by beach lovers.

At the end of the town we joined a newly opened section of the developing England Coast Path, a proposed long-distance National Trail which will follow the coastline of England. When complete in 2020, it will be 2,795 miles in length. After 5 miles, the path reached an Army training area which we were not able to enter, so we had no option by to leave the seafront and head inland for 3 miles to reach Lydd. Maureen was struggling with her other sore 'bits', so we visited a chemist there for some magic cream to appease her discomfort. We also took the opportunity to shop at a nearby supermarket to pick up food for lunch.

The sun was starting to break through as we followed a lane for 2 miles until reaching our next footpath. We found our way blocked by knee-high nettles that swamped the path so much that it was totally impassable. A quick consultation with the OS map and a route round it was identified. This led to crop fields which were equally difficult to get through, with plants almost head-high at times, the farmer having made no attempt to keep the path clear. It was a hassle we could do without, but eventually we had pushed our way through to emerge at New Romney. The local church yard provided a welcome place for a lunch stop.

On resuming we walked through the town before turning right down a long, straight lane leading back to the seafront. On the way, we passed the entrance to the Romney, Hythe and Dymchurch Railway, on which 1/3 size steam and diesel locomotives travel a 13½ miles route between Hythe and

Dungeness. We would later see it in action as it passed close behind our B&B in Dymchurch.

The final 3 miles or so were back on the coastal path running directly behind the beach. It was still very windy on the coast, but the sun had not reappeared, and the temperature was in the mid to low 20's, so a much more comfortable day for walking than recently. A couple of miles further at St Mary's Bay we came across a beach-side coffee shop, where we stopped for a few minutes for a coffee and to take in the views. Soon after we were approaching Dymchurch where several holiday makers were enjoying a stroll along the seafront promenade. A couple made the mistake of doing this with their recently purchased fish and chips in a tray, the food pointing invitingly towards the sky, which the local seagulls were unable to resist. They did no more than swoop down and snatch chips out of the tray as the couple tried in vain to keep the birds at bay. This dispelled any thoughts we had off having a fish and chip supper looking out to sea, opting to pick up some food to eat later outside the B&B.

We arrived at the B&B in better shape than the previous day, though still quite weary, and were pleased to find a relaxed atmosphere on arrival and a lovely room to collapse into. After freshening up we checked our messages. Diana from the Country Walking Facebook Group, who first made contact a few days ago, had been in touch again. She works at our destination, Dover Castle. The castle is managed by English Heritage who had been brilliant when I contacted them earlier in the year with my request for access to the castle grounds. They very kindly sent me four complimentary tickets to the grounds and castle for myself, Maureen, her Auntie Jean and Uncle Jack, who would be meeting us as we finished in Dover. They would also be giving us a ride back home to Derby. Diana confirmed arrangements had been made for us to be met on arrival and escorted to the top of the castle for our grand finale. Let's hope it all goes according to plan!

For now, we needed to recover and refuel, so we took our food out onto the B&B patio, which overlooked a picturesque canal, with views beyond to the wide, open pastures that constitute Romney Marsh. Before too long a familiar whistle alerted us to the miniature train passing by on its last run of the day.

As we sat there I reflected on how fortunate we'd been to get to this point without injury or any significant health problems. Despite Maureen's obvious discomfort we were both in a reasonable condition, albeit tired. Route finding had gone incredibly well, the terrains had mostly been good to walk on and most of the cows we'd come across had let us proceed unhindered. The weather, overall, had been kind with just 8 days of rain so far, although the recent excessive heat was proving a challenge. My boots that I feared would be a problem after a split where the sole bends, had made it okay after all. All hail to King Salomon and his amazing footwear! Our final day tomorrow would be one of mixed emotions, not wanting this incredible journey to end, but keen to be successful in our quest to walk the length of the UK. We can make it, I thought to myself. Just one more huge effort and we'd be in Dover.

Our final day dawned, Thursday 21st July 2016, day 78 of 78, the last 17.5 miles of an incredible 1,041. We had awoken quite early, partly out of excitement and partly to get on the road as soon as possible. Late last night we watched the weather forecast, which showed the south-east corner of the UK in deep red, with 30 degrees expected and little in the way of wind. Not exactly ideal walking conditions, but better than torrential rain! To help Maureen on the last day I again organised for a taxi to take her rucksack onto our next B&B. It might seem extravagant, but there was no point in her carrying it, with the likely adverse effect it would have on her physically and psychologically. With the excellent support, we'd had with her rucksack from friends, plus a couple of taxis, she hadn't had to carry it for any of the last 9 days, which would have been a major struggle in the conditions we'd encountered.

After a quick breakfast, we were on the road by 8.25am. Perversely, we started by heading westwards, back towards Dymchurch town, as we'd been advised that the quickest way to the seafront path was through a passageway a little way down the road. Sure, enough it was soon found and after passing between a few rows of houses we were at the sea wall, on top of which the path is located.

All went well for the first 2 miles, the sun to our right hanging in the clear sky over the dazzling blue sea. We came to the Dymchurch Redoubt, a large circular fortification built between 1798 and 1809 to support a chain of 21 Martello Towers between here and Rye, and to act as a supply depot for them. From this point the next 2 miles is an army firing range and today they were making use of it. There was a guard at the entrance and he wasn't letting anyone through onto the coastal path, so we had no choice but to return to the main road and follow it into Hythe. The sound of guns firing accompanied us down the road, along with the traffic, so this stretch was turning out to be memorable for its noise! Once in the town centre and clear of the 'danger zone', as marked on the OS map, we could turn right down a side street to return to the sea wall path. Our detour had added an extra half mile, ordinarily nothing that would trouble us, but in the escalating heat we could do without any extra distance whatsoever to our final day.

The sea front was a pleasant affair for the next few miles, the calm sea more like an enormous duck pond, with only a steady trickle of people sharing the promenade with us. As we came to

Sandgate a sea front cafe unconsciously beckoned us to take a seat outside, lay down our rucksacks, order a couple of coffees and take in the scenery...so we did. It was a delightful spot that we could have enjoyed for much longer than we stayed, but we'd only done 7 miles so far with plenty of walking still to do.

As we resumed our coastal walking the path travelled past Folkestone, a sizable town with an impressive harbour bustling with people seeking their lunch. Buying fish and chips here was not a difficulty, with plenty of outlets, but we resisted the temptation. Once past the many boats moored in the harbour, we were on the east side of town and soon came to the harbour church. Here we located a flight of steps to take us up towards yet another Martello Tower and along an expanse of cliff top grass, where we spotted a bench ideally situated for a short break.

"It's so hot", exclaimed Maureen. "I'm so grateful for a sit down. I didn't imagine it would be as tough as this over these last few days".

"Neither did I", I agreed. "I realise it's July and were in the south-east, but I didn't expect temperatures of around 28 degrees, as the weather app on my mobile phone indicates it is. Keep drinking plenty of water", I urged.

Our path now rose steeply to reach the top of East Cliff and the Warren Country Park, from where extensive views along the coast to Dover were possible. After this there would only be one more significant climb left to do, up to Dover Castle. The path serves two purposes at this point, being both the Saxon Shore Way once again, but also part of the North Downs Way. We continued along the undulating cliff top passing behind the Eurotunnel terminal, populated by those seeking a ride under the English Channel to France. The terminal is situated on the west side of Dover, ostensibly to keep it well away from the busy ferry ports I imagined, but there may be a more geological, engineering based reason for its location, truth be known.

Once beyond the terminal we gained our first clear sight of Dover and a glimpse of the distant castle, mounted traditionally high, overseeing its surrounding area. At 15 miles the path turned inland, but not before overlooking the cruise liner terminal and the main Dover docks. It was a hive of activity down there and we were relived not to be embroiled in the hustle and bustle. After bypassing what remains of the Drop Redoubt fortification, we went down a set of steps and suddenly found ourselves doing something very ordinary – standing by the kerb waiting for the pelican crossing to allow us to cross a busy road. It seemed weird to be doing this after so long on the coast and away from such simple aspects of everyday life.

It felt even hotter in the town. We were a little ahead of time for meeting up with Jean and Jack, so we decided to stop for a healthy lunch in the curiously named Beano Cafe. There's no obvious connection between Folkestone and the famous children's comic, plus the cafe owners were Italian with seemingly no natural affinity with the characters displayed on the walls. Once replenished it was time for the last lap, the final push for journey's end.

"Looks like we're going to make it, Maureen", I said. "Are you ready for the grand finale?"

"You bet", she said, with both excitement and a look of relief on her face at the same time.

It was just half a mile across the town to get to our B&B, the appropriately named Castle Guest House, which I'd booked in the knowledge that we would have to walk right past it on our way up to Dover Castle. I'd also booked a room there for Jean and Jack, with the plan being to meet them outside and walk up to the castle together. We turned a corner into Castle Hill Road and immediately spotted Jean waving her arms aloft, with Jack as ever by her side. They greeted us warmly with hugs and handshakes.

We now had just half a mile more to complete! The four of us set off on the steep ascent up Castle Hill Road, soon reaching a driveway entrance to the castle grounds on our right where a small hut served as the gate reception.

"Hi", I said to the lady attendant, "Diana from the Admin Office is expecting us and asked that you call her upon our arrival please".

"Sure, no problem", she replied and soon came back to say that Diana would be along in a few minutes. Almost instantaneously she was walking towards us with her colleagues Kirsty and Rachel. Together they were holding a large poster that read "Welcome to Dover Castle - Well Done Team Shipley!" What a brilliant surprise and very much appreciated. The first of many photos were taken before our guides proceeded to take us up through the grounds on a winding, gradual incline until we were at the castle itself. It's an impressive structure, one of the largest Norman castles in England, which has stood on this site since the year 1180 AD. An amazing amount of history has taken place here over the last 2,000 years. Now 'Maureen and Martin' were here to create a little piece of history of their own!

"We know you've had a long day, but we thought you might like to finish your epic journey on the roof of the castle. It will mean a few stairs, if that's okay?" said Kirsty.

"Perfect, let's do it", I said. Off we went through the intricate stairways inside the castle, pausing at a huge throne to sit and have further photos taken, before the last dozen steps took us through an opening onto the roof. A Union Jack flag was flying and as I'd always hoped and envisaged, we were high aloft over

Dover, with views out to sea, feeling fantastic at completing our walk.

It had been the most incredible experience for the last 78 days since we left Cape Wrath on 5th May, almost 3 months ago. We had seen first-hand some of the UK's finest scenery and we'd met many wonderful people along the way on our 1,041-mile journey. We had walked side by side, supporting each other every step of the way and were still on speaking terms at the end of it all! Our many, many generous supporters had donated an amazing £3,332 for Thrombosis UK in memory of Dawn, Maureen's greatly missed daughter and my step daughter, who left us all too soon in 2011. Theirs and numerous other messages of support had been a tremendous boost to us throughout our journey.

But most of all the memories we'd created during our walk will stay with us forever, both the wonderful times and the more challenging aspects, all of which go to make the UK the diverse and excellent place that it is.

Here at Dover our epic journey had come to an end. We had indeed, made it! It had truly been 'A Bit Of A Caper'.

With Becky, Jacqueline, Sally, Chris and Jane on the SDW.

The wonderful Seven Sisters on the SDW.

Martin and Bev admire the Eastbourne beach huts.

A scorcher on the sea front with Nicola.

The end is in sight – Dover Castle and the last climb beckon.

Kirsty and Diana greet us at Dover Castle.

Appendix – Detailed Route Map
Cape Wrath to Dover – 5th May to 21st July 2016

(data format = walking day & date – location **reached** – miles walked – cumulative mileage)

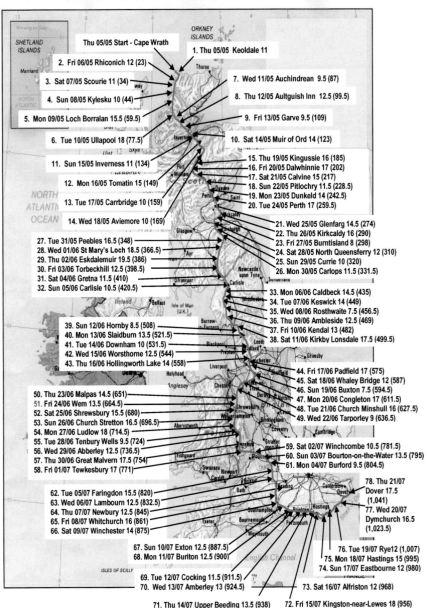

Thu 05/05 Start - Cape Wrath

1. Thu 05/05 Keoldale 11
2. Fri 06/05 Rhiconich 12 (23)
3. Sat 07/05 Scourie 11 (34)
4. Sun 08/05 Kylesku 10 (44)
5. Mon 09/05 Loch Borralan 15.5 (59.5)
6. Tue 10/05 Ullapool 18 (77.5)
7. Wed 11/05 Auchindrean 9.5 (87)
8. Thu 12/05 Aultguish Inn 12.5 (99.5)
9. Fri 13/05 Garve 9.5 (109)
10. Sat 14/05 Muir of Ord 14 (123)
11. Sun 15/05 Inverness 11 (134)
12. Mon 16/05 Tomatin 15 (149)
13. Tue 17/05 Carrbridge 10 (159)
14. Wed 18/05 Aviemore 10 (169)
15. Thu 19/05 Kingussie 16 (185)
16. Fri 20/05 Dalwhinnie 17 (202)
17. Sat 21/05 Calvine 15 (217)
18. Sun 22/05 Pitlochry 11.5 (228.5)
19. Mon 23/05 Dunkeld 14 (242.5)
20. Tue 24/05 Perth 17 (259.5)
21. Wed 25/05 Glenfarg 14.5 (274)
22. Thu 26/05 Kirkcaldy 16 (290)
23. Fri 27/05 Burntisland 8 (298)
24. Sat 28/05 North Queensferry 12 (310)
25. Sun 29/05 Currie 10 (320)
26. Mon 30/05 Carlops 11.5 (331.5)
27. Tue 31/05 Peebles 16.5 (348)
28. Wed 01/06 St Mary's Loch 18.5 (366.5)
29. Thu 02/06 Eskdalemuir 19.5 (386)
30. Fri 03/06 Torbeckhill 12.5 (398.5)
31. Sat 04/06 Gretna 11.5 (410)
32. Sun 05/06 Carlisle 10.5 (420.5)
33. Mon 06/06 Caldbeck 14.5 (435)
34. Tue 07/06 Keswick 14 (449)
35. Wed 08/06 Rosthwaite 7.5 (456.5)
36. Thu 09/06 Ambleside 12.5 (469)
37. Fri 10/06 Kendal 13 (482)
38. Sat 11/06 Kirkby Lonsdale 17.5 (499.5)
39. Sun 12/06 Hornby 8.5 (508)
40. Mon 13/06 Slaidburn 13.5 (521.5)
41. Tue 14/06 Downham 10 (531.5)
42. Wed 15/06 Worsthorne 12.5 (544)
43. Thu 16/06 Hollingworth Lake 14 (558)
44. Fri 17/06 Padfield 17 (575)
45. Sat 18/06 Whaley Bridge 12 (587)
46. Sun 19/06 Buxton 7.5 (594.5)
47. Mon 20/06 Congleton 17 (611.5)
48. Tue 21/06 Church Minshull 16 (627.5)
49. Wed 22/06 Tarporley 9 (636.5)
50. Thu 23/06 Malpas 14.5 (651)
51. Fri 24/06 Wem 13.5 (664.5)
52. Sat 25/06 Shrewsbury 15.5 (680)
53. Sun 26/06 Church Stretton 16.5 (696.5)
54. Mon 27/06 Ludlow 18 (714.5)
55. Tue 28/06 Tenbury Wells 9.5 (724)
56. Wed 29/06 Abberley 12.5 (736.5)
57. Thu 30/06 Great Malvern 17.5 (754)
58. Fri 01/07 Tewkesbury 17 (771)
59. Sat 02/07 Winchcombe 10.5 (781.5)
60. Sun 03/07 Bourton-on-the-Water 13.5 (795)
61. Mon 04/07 Burford 9.5 (804.5)
62. Tue 05/07 Faringdon 15.5 (820)
63. Wed 06/07 Lambourn 12.5 (832.5)
64. Thu 07/07 Newbury 12.5 (845)
65. Fri 08/07 Whitchurch 16 (861)
66. Sat 09/07 Winchester 14 (875)
67. Sun 10/07 Exton 12.5 (887.5)
68. Mon 11/07 Buriton 12.5 (900)
69. Tue 12/07 Cocking 11.5 (911.5)
70. Wed 13/07 Amberley 13 (924.5)
71. Thu 14/07 Upper Beeding 13.5 (938)
72. Fri 15/07 Kingston-near-Lewes 18 (956)
73. Sat 16/07 Alfriston 12 (968)
74. Sun 17/07 Eastbourne 12 (980)
75. Mon 18/07 Hastings 15 (995)
76. Tue 19/07 Rye12 (1,007)
77. Wed 20/07 Dymchurch 16.5 (1,023.5)
78. Thu 21/07 Dover 17.5 (1,041)

245

Appendix – Walk Itinerary

Walk Day	Day of Week	Date	From – To	Miles	Total Walked
1	Thursday	05/05/16	Cape Wrath - Keoldale	11	11
2	Friday	06/05/16	Keoldale - Rhiconich	12	23
3	Saturday	07/05/16	Rhiconich - Scourie	11	34
4	Sunday	08/05/16	Scourie - Kylesku	10	44
5	Monday	09/05/16	Kylesku - Loch Borralan	15.5	59.5
6	Tuesday	10/05/16	Loch Borralan - Ullapool	18	77.5
7	Wednesday	11/05/16	Ullapool - Auchindrean	9.5	87
8	Thursday	12/05/16	Auchindrean - Aultguish Inn	12.5	99.5
9	Friday	13/05/16	Aultguish Inn - Garve	9.5	109
10	Saturday	14/05/16	Garve - Muir of Ord	14	123
11	Sunday	15/05/16	Muir of Ord -Inverness	11	134
12	Monday	16/05/16	Inverness - Tomatin	15	149
13	Tuesday	17/05/16	Tomatin - Carrbridge	10	159
14	Wednesday	18/05/16	Carrbridge - Aviemore	10	169
15	Thursday	19/05/16	Aviemore - Kingussie	16	185
16	Friday	20/05/16	Kingussie - Dalwhinnie	17	202
17	Saturday	21/05/16	Dalwhinnie - Calvine	15	217
18	Sunday	22/05/16	Calvine - Pitlochry	11.5	228.5
19	Monday	23/05/16	Pitlochry - Dunkeld	14	242.5
20	Tuesday	24/05/16	Dunkeld - Perth	17	259.5
21	Wednesday	25/05/16	Perth - Glenfarg	14.5	274
22	Thursday	26/05/16	Glenfarg - Kirkcaldy	16	290
23	Friday	27/05/16	Kirkcaldy - Burntisland	8	298
24	Saturday	28/05/16	Burntisland - North Queensferry	12	310
25	Sunday	29/05/16	North Queensferry - Currie (12 miles)	10	320
26	Monday	30/05/16	Currie - Carlops	11.5	331.5
27	Tuesday	31/05/16	Carlops - Peebles	16.5	348
28	Wednesday	01/06/16	Peebles-St Mary's		
28	Wednesday	01/06/16	Peebles - St Mary's Loch	18.5	366.5
29	Thursday	02/06/16	St Mary's Loch - Eskdalemuir	19.5	386
30	Friday	03/06/16	Eskdalemuir - Torbeckhill	12.5	398.5

Walk Day	Day of Week	Date	From – To	Miles	Total Walked
31	Saturday	04/06/16	Torbeckhill - Gretna	11.5	410
32	Sunday	05/06/16	Gretna - Carlisle	10.5	420.5
33	Monday	06/06/16	Carlisle - Caldbeck	14.5	435
34	Tuesday	07/06/16	Caldbeck - Keswick	14	449
35	Wednesday	08/06/16	Keswick - Rosthwaite	7.5	456.5
36	Thursday	09/06/16	Rosthwaite - Ambleside	12.5	469
37	Friday	10/06/16	Ambleside - Kendal	13	482
38	Saturday	11/06/16	Kendal - Kirkby Lonsdale	17.5	499.5
39	Sunday	12/06/16	Kirkby Lonsdale - Hornby	8.5	508
40	Monday	13/06/16	Hornby - Slaidburn	13.5	521.5
41	Tuesday	14/06/16	Slaidburn - Downham	10	531.5
42	Wednesday	15/06/16	Downham - Worsthorne	12.5	544
43	Thursday	16/06/16	Worsthorne - Hollingworh Lake	14	558
44	Friday	17/06/16	Hollingworth Lake - Padfield	17	575
45	Saturday	18/06/16	Padfield - Whaley Bridge	12	587
46	Sunday	19/06/16	Whaley Bridge - Buxton	7.5	594.5
47	Monday	20/06/16	Buxton - Congleton	17	611.5
48	Tuesday	21/06/16	Congleton - Church Minshull	16	627.5
49	Wednesday	22/06/16	Church Minshull - Tarporley	9	636.5
50	Thursday	23/06/16	Tarporley - Malpas	14.5	651
51	Friday	24/06/16	Malpas - Wem	13.5	664.5
52	Saturday	25/06/16	Wem - Shrewsbury	15.5	680
53	Sunday	26/06/16	Shrewsbury - Church Stretton	16.5	696.5
54	Monday	27/06/16	Church Stretton - Ludlow	18	714.5
55	Tuesday	28/06/16	Ludlow - Tenbury Wells	9.5	724
56	Wednesday	29/06/16	Tenbury Wells - Abberley	12.5	736.5

Walk Day	Day of Week	Date	From – To	Miles	Total Walked
57	Thursday	30/06/16	Abberley - Great Malvern	17.5	754
58	Friday	01/07/16	Great Malvern - Tewkesbury	17	771
59	Saturday	02/07/16	Tewkesbury - Winchcombe	10.5	781.5
60	Sunday	03/07/16	Winchcombe - Bourton-on-the-Water	13.5	795
61	Monday	04/07/16	Bourton-on-the-Water - Burford	9.5	804.5
62	Tuesday	05/07/16	Burford - Faringdon	15.5	820
63	Wednesday	06/07/16	Faringdon - Lambourn	12.5	832.5
64	Thursday	07/07/16	Lambourn - Newbury	12.5	845
65	Friday	08/07/16	Newbury - Whitchurch	16	861
66	Saturday	09/07/16	Whitchurch - Winchester	14	875
67	Sunday	10/07/16	Winchester - Exton	12.5	887.5
68	Monday	11/07/16	Exton - Buriton	12.5	900
69	Tuesday	12/07/16	Buriton - Cocking	11.5	911.5
70	Wednesday	13/07/16	Cocking - Amberley	13	924.5
71	Thursday	14/07/16	Amberley - Upper Beeding	13.5	938
72	Friday	15/07/16	Upper Beeding - Kingston-near-Lewes	18	956
73	Saturday	16/07/16	Kingston-near-Lewes - Alfriston	12	968
74	Sunday	17/07/16	Alfriston - Eastbourne	12	980
75	Monday	18/07/16	Eastbourne - Hastings	15	995
76	Tuesday	19/07/16	Hastings - Rye	12	1007
77	Wednesday	20/07/16	Rye - Dymchurch	16.5	1023.5
78	Thursday	21/07/16	Dymchurch - Dover	17.5	1041

Appendix - Baggage Transfer Heroes

Tuesday 10th May	Loch Borralan to Ullapool	Lesley Sherman
Monday 23rd May	Pitlochry to Dunkeld	Anne Stewart
Wednesday 25th May	Green of Invermay to Glenfarg (part)	Rupert Hutchinson
Wednesday 1st June	Peebles to Hartleap (part)	Lindsay Lewis
Tuesday 7th June	Caldbeck to Keswick	Brigantes baggage company
Saturday 11th June	Kendal to Kirkby Lonsdale	Taxi
Thursday 16th June	Worsthorne to Hollingworth Lake	Frances Ipson
Saturday 18th June	Padfield to Whaley Bridge	Lindsay Pulley
Sunday 19th June	Whaley Bridge to Buxton	Julian & Wendy Barron
Tuesday 21st June	Congleton to Church Minshull	Helen Taylor
Sunday 26th June	Shrewsbury to Church Stretton	Taxi
Monday 27th June	Church Stretton to Ludlow	Diane Chadwick
Tuesday 28th June	Ludlow to Tenbury Wells	Gaynor Davies
Thursday 30th June	Abberley to Great Malvern	Kate Arthur
Friday 1st July	Great Malvern to Tewkesbury	Kate Arthur
Sunday 3rd July	Winchcombe to Bourton-on-the-Water	Tim Dalton
Thursday 7th July	Lambourn to Newbury	Pam Clark
Friday 8th July	Newbury to Whitchurch	Pam Clark
Wednesday 13th July	Cocking to Amberley	Keren Rees
Thursday 14th July	Amberley to Upper Beeding	Jacqueline Gale
Friday 15th July	Upper Beeding to Kingston	Jacqueline Gale
Saturday 16th July	Kingston to Alfriston	Nicola Godin
Sunday 17th July	Alfriston to Eastbourne	Nicola Godin
Monday 18th July	Eastbourne to Hastings	Bev Wood
Tuesday 19th July	Hastings to Rye	Andrew White
Wednesday 20th July	Rye to Dymchurch	Taxi
Thursday 21st July	Dymchurch to Dover	Taxi